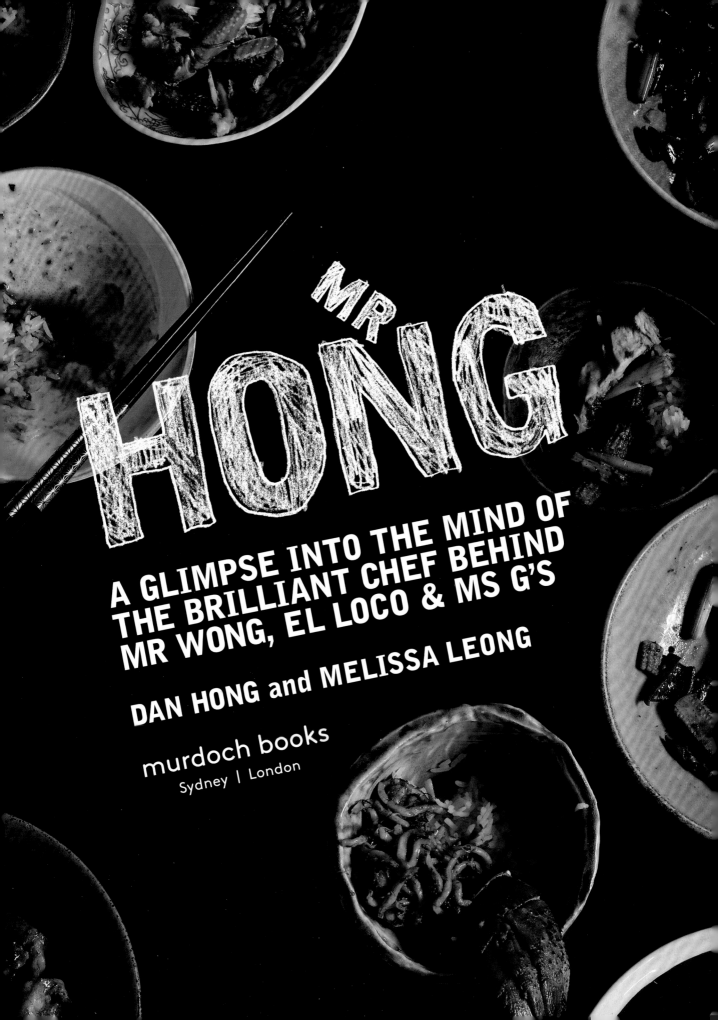

MR HONG

A GLIMPSE INTO THE MIND OF THE BRILLIANT CHEF BEHIND MR WONG, EL LOCO & MS G'S

DAN HONG and MELISSA LEONG

murdoch books

Sydney | London

FOREWORD

This last summer as I was sitting on the floor of my son Daniel's apartment playing with my almost one-year-old granddaughter Namira, I found myself wondering what she will be like when she gets older. What will she want to do for work? Will she have Daniel's attitude and passion for life? (As a Vietnamese grandmother, it is never too early to wonder these things.) Daniel, for most of his teenage years, didn't know what he wanted to do for a career.

He grew up in the '80s in the northern suburbs of Sydney when there was a huge influx of migrants to Australia, particularly from South East Asia. Due to my work as a translator, Daniel and his two sisters, Francoise and Rebecca, were left to their own devices from a young age to fend for themselves in the kitchen. I'd marinate chicken in lemongrass, chilli and garlic and leave it in the fridge before I left for work, and they'd come home from school, figure out how to cook it, steam rice and feed themselves (this may have also been the time Daniel discovered his love of the frozen food aisle at the supermarket). What they missed in family company during the week, we made up for every Sunday with visits to Cabramatta where large family feasts at their grandparents' house would take place. Here, traditional Vietnamese cuisine blended with our French heritage and meals included everything from perfect terrines and pâtés to very traditional Vietnamese soups and stews of offal, blood jelly and plenty of chilli. Frequent trips with the kids back to Vietnam also opened up their eyes to the world of food, and I believe those experiences really helped to shape Daniel's palate.

It wasn't just about the food of our culture. As the kids grew older and Sydney became even more multicultural, our family outings for food took us around the world. On rare nights when I wasn't working at my restaurant in Cabramatta or Newtown, we would travel to Turkey one night, Laos the next, followed by Lebanese, Chinese, and even the occasional fine diner.

I noticed through these early years, Daniel's natural interest in being in the kitchen (as well as his love for eating), so I suggested to him that he might do a cooking apprenticeship. Now, after dedicating over a decade and a half to the kitchen, my son has become a successful chef, known for his innovative and dynamic approach.

I will admit that Daniel was not an easy child to raise, and him asking me to write this foreword may be my only opportunity to tell the world how much heartache he gave me! But when he told me he didn't know what he wanted to do after high school was over, I told him I didn't mind so long as he worked hard and followed his passion… otherwise, it is a waste of time. This is the way Daniel's father, Le, and I both approached parenting. He would say to all of them, 'Work hard, love each other and be happy.' And while our family unit has changed over the years, as a role model, he always leads by example.

I believe Daniel's success is a combination of hard work, determination and a fearless approach to discovering new ideas and using them to create his own way. Cooking has become the most honest way he communicates his personality, his feelings and his ideas. As a parent, all you can hope for is for your child to find themselves and be at peace with who they are… and I'm so proud (and relieved) that Daniel has managed to find that for himself.

Angie Hong

INTRODUCTION

I wasn't really sure what to call this book. Most of the cookbooks and food books that I admire are named after the chef's first restaurant, but I can't really do that… because I don't technically have one. Instead, I seem to have found myself in the position of being responsible for creating the ideas for, and (in a way) giving birth to, a handful of restaurants based in Sydney, Australia. From sorta-Mexican (El Loco), to Chinese (Mr Wong) and modern Asian (Ms G's), they each have a distinct DNA – the experiences they give people are completely different, from look to feel and most importantly, taste. The one thing they do have in common though, is that they're all about big flavours, and above all things, fun.

The food I create at each venue comes from my own mixture of life experiences, from growing up in my mum's Vietnamese restaurant, Thanh Binh, in Cabramatta, to experimenting with supermarket staples while left at home to my own devices during high school, and later, my culinary training at some of Australia's best restaurants. It's been an unlikely progression of events, to say the least. I also tend to get a bit obsessive about particular kinds of food and my mates and I go out on mammoth eating missions trying to find the best ramen, Korean fried chicken or burgers. When I find a dish I like, I eat it, research it, eat it, break it down until I can understand what makes it tick and, lastly, I eat it again (and again, and again).

While many of the recipes in this book can be found on the menu at the restaurants I created them for, this book isn't about a restaurant concept, or a single type of cuisine. It's more about a collection of stories from my life to date. The idea is that by sharing it with you, you'll get a window into how I create the food that I do. I grew up in the suburbs. I didn't do that well at school. I like sneakers, rap and am a shamelessly big eater. I don't think I'm an overly outspoken person, but I think that cooking is my way of expressing my emotions. My families – my real one, my work one and my friends – make me who I am. And it's the lessons they've taught me that have allowed me to see food as something that connects people, makes them happy, and that should be shared with the people in your life.

The food in this book is the stuff I like to cook, eat and share. I come from a fine dining culinary background, but along the journey to working out my own personal cooking style, I found that what made sense to me didn't relate to anything molecular or even highly technical. It's relaxed, should be enjoyed in company, the flavours should punch you in the face (and you'll like it). Like the food of my Vietnamese heritage, it's about bold, strong flavours, freshness and balance. There are a few guilty pleasures thrown in for good measure (handy for hangovers, late night pantry raids or grossing out health-obsessed friends). There are also useful tips that you can use in your own culinary journey to help you develop your own style. In short, this book is about food you want to eat. And I hope you do.

STUFF YOU'RE GOING TO NEED

There's nothing worse than getting started on a recipe and realising you don't have the right equipment. Chefs have all the toys, so it can sometimes be a challenge for a home cook to replicate restaurant recipes in their own kitchen. You don't need to have a Pacojet or a Thermomix at home, but there are a few key pieces of equipment you'll find handy when cooking recipes from this book.

A STUPIDLY LARGE STOCKPOT

Stocks are my thing. And learning how to get them right can make a huge difference to your cooking. A lot of these stock recipes call for a fair few ingredients and, by the time you stuff everything into a medium-sized saucepan, there may not be any space left for water. My advice is to buy the biggest stockpot you have room for. You can usually find commercial kitchen suppliers that will sell you a small tiger pot or something similar. If not, feel free to reduce the quantities of ingredients in the same proportions and make less stock.

A CLIP-ON MEAT THERMOMETER

In the restaurant, we measure things by temperature to get a consistent and accurate end result. A meat thermometer is a very handy thing to own, especially when deep-frying or checking the internal temperature of a piece of meat. If you don't have an immersion circulator, a thermometer is also handy in slow cooking eggs.

A GOOD SET OF STRAINERS

A set of strainers with different sizes of mesh – from large to fine – are useful for making crystal-clear stocks. Larger mesh strainers are handy to remove vegetables and herbs, while finer strainers are great for catching smaller particles and skimming fat from the surface of your stock or broth.

A HAND-HELD BLENDER/FOOD PROCESSOR
These days, plenty of brands do a good home food-processing kit, which has everything from a dough hook to a liquidiser and a good general chopping tool. Get one.

A DIGITAL SCALE
There are times when a recipe requires something more precise than cups or tablespoons and it's better to measure ingredients in grams. A digital scale can help you be a bit more accurate when executing a recipe at home.

JARS
There are a few recipes, such as nuoc cham, pickles and XO sauce, which can be made in batches and stored in the fridge to be used whenever. It's always handy to have a couple of spare jam jars or bottles to manage this.

A GOOD, HEAVY-BASED SAUCEPAN
A lot of recipes call for deep-frying or high heat, so a quality saucepan that will cope with a bit of a beating is something anyone who likes to cook should own.

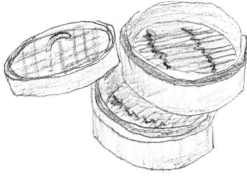

STEAMER BASKETS
Any good Asian kitchen will need a heap of bamboo steamer baskets. Luckily they're super cheap. Invest in a range of sizes, and check that you can fit your bowls or plates inside and secure the lid. Handy for everything from the chawanmushi-style mapo tofu, to steamed oysters and fish.

BIG MIXING BOWLS
Nothing is more inconvenient than trying to mix things in a bowl that is too small. You'll be surprised how many uses you'll have for them when you own a good range of large mixing bowls. Pick up cheap stainless steel ones from commercial cooking suppliers.

PANTRY MUST-HAVES

CONDIMENTS

You can tell how keen a cook someone is by how many condiments they keep in their cupboard. Oils, vinegars and sauces are the key to good Asian cooking and there are a few that you should invest in as a lot of recipes in this book call for specific Asian food brands. It is totally fine to use another brand if you prefer, or if you can't find the one listed. That's the other thing about Asian cooking – you use what you have and tweak it to suit your own personal taste: everyone is different.

| OYSTER SAUCE | DARK SOY SAUCE | XANTHAN GUM | LIGHT SOY SAUCE | SOY PASTE | ROCK SUGAR | MIRIN |

| VEGETABLE OIL | FISH SAUCE | SHIRO-DASHI | CHINESE RED VINEGAR | JAPANESE SOY SAUCE | WHITE VINEGAR | WHITE SOY SAUCE | YUZUKOSHŌ |

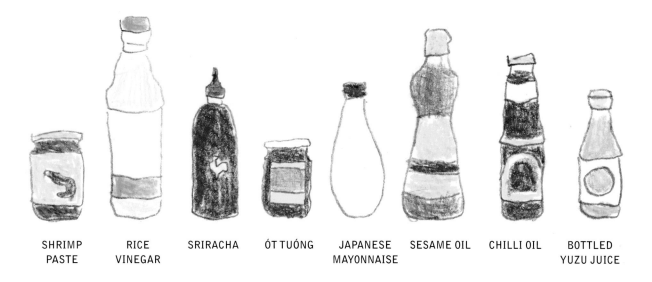

| SHRIMP PASTE | RICE VINEGAR | SRIRACHA | ÓT TUÓNG | JAPANESE MAYONNAISE | SESAME OIL | CHILLI OIL | BOTTLED YUZU JUICE |

| LAO GAN MA CHILLI OIL | CHINKIANG BLACK VINEGAR | KNORR LIQUID SEASONING | COOKING SAKE | KOMBU EXTRACT | SHAOXING COOKING WINE | HOISIN SAUCE |

FRESH INGREDIENTS

BROWN ONIONS

CHILLIES
(both bird's eye and small long red chillies)

CORIANDER
(cilantro)

GARLIC

GINGER

SPRING ONIONS
(scallions)

CHAPTER ONE

THE PENNY DROPS

Instead of starting at the start (which would be far too logical), I thought I'd start at the point in my life that really made everything fall into place – that moment when the penny dropped and I started to understand more about my cooking style and, importantly, more about myself, too.

That penny-dropping moment happened when I was working at Lotus in Sydney's Potts Point in March 2008. I'd taken over the head chef position from Lauren Murdoch, a really well respected chef with a similar background to mine in European technique. Lotus had a dedicated following. There was also a real traditional sense of formality, with the menu divided into entrées, mains and desserts. At that time I was still figuring out my style as a chef, and I felt in a lot of ways that Lotus was tired and lacked a distinct identity. Here I was cooking food that wasn't really mine, and didn't really belong to the two previous chefs that cooked there either.

While I was starting to figure out my own style, I discovered that a group of peers was trying to communicate their own ideas as well. Frustrated by the confines of the restaurant format, we decided to express ourselves by putting on a series of dining events that pushed the envelope and allowed us to collaborate. This crew consisted of chefs, sommeliers, front-of-house, bartenders, musicians, designers, photographers and a promoter, to pull it all together. And so, [TOYS] collective (Taste of Young Sydney), was born. It was an exciting time for us and it seemed that the industry was hungry to see things like this happen. We announced our first dinner and, to our surprise, it sold out in a matter of hours. Each event had a theme to tie everything together and was designed to push both ourselves and our guests outside of comfort zones, but also not to be taken too seriously. For our first theme, Phat, I did a dish inspired by the life and times of the Notorious B.I.G., complete with corn purée and fried chicken wings (humble beginnings), to foie gras (less humble), and 'blood splatter' of beetroot and raspberry (his not-so-happy ending).

Through [TOYS] collective, we began to discover ourselves, and a new network of industry friends who were trying to do the same things: be free to express our creative ideas, be successful and have fun doing it. In a way, the people [TOYS] attracted as members were always going to do well, but I think doing what we did together fast-tracked our trajectories beyond our expectations. I look at the crew now and they're opening restaurants overseas, winning awards and even mentoring new blood. I don't think the conditions will ever be the same as they were then, but I'm glad to have been a part of it.

Then David Chang happened. The Momofuku book had just dropped and David was about to arrive in Australia to be a part of the Melbourne Food and Wine Festival. At that time (and to date), chefs such as David were the heroes of our global food scene. The whole 'take no prisoners' and 'cook whatever the hell you feel like so long as it's true' approach really made people wake up to the new reality of eating… and Frank Roberts (the Group Restaurant Manager for Merivale, of which Lotus was a part) suggested I cook a Momofuku dinner with David. To my excitement, he agreed, and it was all systems go.

That evening – 25 March 2010 – was a real turning point in my career. The dinner sold out soon after it was announced and, interestingly, friends from Sydney's restaurant scene bought the majority of tickets. Critics, chefs, sommeliers… everyone wanted to be there. For some reason, the idea of me cooking David's food resonated with them… and, when I talk to people who were there that night, they still remember it clearly.

The pressure to pull this dinner off was huge, but David was really cool about it. After agreeing to do the dinner, I emailed him and asked, 'What do you want me to do?' He said: 'You decide. You have the cookbook.' I wrote up the menu, he gave it the thumbs up and we just executed what we'd chosen from the book. David arrived on the day, tasted everything and to our relief he just said: 'Great!'

On the day, Justin Hemmes (Merivale's man in charge, visionary and friend) told me he was coming in at 5 pm and that I had one hour to cook him the whole dinner from start to finish, as he had to be elsewhere soon after (no pressure). Naturally we did, and he left smiling. Then the real dinner started. From the get-go, it was a winner. We played loud music (David had brought his iPod so we could blast the playlist from Momofuku), cooked ridiculously tasty food and everyone basically lost their shit. The vibe was exactly as I'd wanted it to be. At some point in the evening, my friend, chef Morgan McGlone got a call from his mate Alex Atala (owner/chef of D.O.M. in Brazil and another culinary legend), who he'd gotten to know in South America. He was also in town and had missed out on his booking at Tetsuya's because he was running late. He wanted to come to Lotus and catch up with David, and asked if we could fit him in. So at this point, we had the chefs and owners of two of the world's best restaurant visionaries in the house AND every major food critic and respected industry peer in attendance (seriously NO PRESSURE!).

After all was said and done, it was one of those magic nights where everything seemed to go right. Everyone I valued and wanted to share the meal with was there, and everything just clicked.

The next day, Justin pulled me aside and said, 'I have an empty site around the corner and I would like you to open a place there. I want it to feel like you and your best mate saved as much money as you could and opened a restaurant – like you did the fit-out and made the furniture yourselves. It should be fun, and have a real sense of personality.' That empty space eventually became Ms G's.

My head chef and one of my closest friends, Jowett Yu and I agreed right away that the restaurant would have to be about food we liked to go out and eat. On our days off, Jow and I go to Chinatown to eat. All we do is talk about Asian food. Who serves the best tonkotsu ramen? Where is the best Korean fried chicken to be found? Or the best burger or Chinese BBQ? So Jow and I decided that if we were going to open a new restaurant, it'd be about using our culinary training backgrounds and combining them with everything we loved to eat… from junk food to Chinatown favourites.

We went on a research trip to New York to get a feel for the kind of vibe and food we wanted to create. Justin, Jow and I ate at all of David's restaurants and I thought how awesome (and liberating) it must be to put whatever you want on a menu. From flavoured soft serves to bacon and kimchi, pork buns or a plate of prosciutto – the one and only constant was that all the food was delicious. Aside from that, there seemed to be an 'anything goes' philosophy. It was an inspiring time for me as a chef, as I have now adopted that approach and deliciousness is now the main driver when it comes to all the food I make. **Deliciousness**. Why aren't chefs cooking the stuff we love to eat when we, as chefs, go out for dinner? If diners look to us for what's making us hungry, surely they want to eat that, too?

When Jow and I got back from New York, and until we opened Ms G's, we decided to start changing the menu at Lotus to make it about food we wanted to eat. If it packed a punch, was indulgent and most of all, super tasty, then we put it on. That's how the Lotus Burger came into being. After eating almost every burger in existence in New York, we became obsessed with how to make the best American-style, greasy, squishy guilty-pleasure burger you could get. At that point in Sydney, the only really good burger around was at Rockpool Bar & Grill. Even so, it was a more dressed-up take on a burger – brioche bun, Zuni pickle, full-blood wagyu patty, bacon and gruyère.

At the other end of the spectrum, there will always be a part of me that loves a dirty hamburger from the local corner shop. But really, there were very few individuals in Australia who knew how to make a proper American-style burger. To add insult to injury, burger joints started to go 'gourmet', using damper buns and adding tomato jam and other ridiculous items to burgers. In my belief, this just takes us further away from what a real burger is.

We wanted to make a dirty burger. Nothing about the Lotus Burger is meant to be 'special'. It's about Heinz Tomato Ketchup, Japanese mayonnaise and processed American cheese… the only things you make are the patty and the caramelised onions. Flick to page 36 for more on the burger.

Easily one of the most popular dishes in the history of Lotus. The sweet wasabi is really what makes this dish. During the height of the elBulli hype, a chef I worked with at Moog had just returned from working there and came up with this emulsion to serve with fish. The heat and sweetness work well with any raw seafood, particularly scallops, scampi or kingfish.

SASHIMI OF TUNA with SWEET WASABI, SOY GINGER DRESSING

Serves 5 as an entrée

1 whole kohlrabi, leaves removed
pickling liquid (Essentials, page 241)

Peel the kohlrabi. This recipe uses the white turnip-like flesh of the vegetable. Cut the flesh into long matchsticks about 5 mm (¼ inch) thick. Transfer the kohlrabi matchsticks to an airtight container and sprinkle with a little salt. Cover and set aside in a cool place overnight.

SWEET WASABI
90 g (3¼ oz/2 tubes) wasabi
1 egg yolk
juice of ½ lime
4 tablespoons honey
½ teaspoon salt
350 ml (12 fl oz) grapeseed oil

This emulsion is similar to a mayonnaise. Put the wasabi, egg yolk, lime juice, honey and salt into the bowl of a food processor. Turn the machine onto a low setting and slowly, very slowly, pour 150 ml (5 fl oz) of oil into the food processor in a steady stream. At this stage, if the mayonnaise gets a little thick, add a little splash of water. Slowly pour in the rest of the oil in a steady stream. The end result should resemble a really thick mayonnaise.

GINGER VINAIGRETTE
1½ tablespoons mirin
100 ml (3½ fl oz) sugar syrup (Essentials, page 240)
100 ml (3½ fl oz) rice wine vinegar
165 ml (5¼ fl oz) light soy sauce
300 ml (10½ fl oz) ginger oil (Essentials, page 238)

Add all ingredients in a bowl with 130 ml (4¼ fl oz) water and mix until well combined. Set aside.

THE REST
5 x 100 g (3½ oz) pieces sashimi-grade tuna, sinew and bloodlines removed
2 spring onions (scallions), thinly sliced
150 g (5½ oz) salted cucumber (Essentials, page 241)
30 g (1 oz) wakame, rehydrated, sliced
baby coriander (cilantro) and baby shiso (perilla) leaves, to garnish
sea salt flakes, to serve

When you are ready to serve the sashimi, use a sharp knife to cut each piece of tuna into 7–8 pieces and transfer to a bowl. Whisk the vinaigrette and pour about 3 tablespoons of it over the tuna. Leave to marinate for 1–2 minutes.

In another bowl, add the spring onions, pickled kohlrabi (drained), salted cucumber and wakame. Gently mix the lot with your hands and divide among five bowls.

TO SERVE

Arrange the marinated tuna pieces on top of the salad and spoon some of the marinade dressing over the fish. Garnish with baby coriander and shiso leaves and sprinkle with a few salt flakes. Finally, spoon some of the sweet wasabi emulsion on the side of the plate for dipping.

HONG HACK
Wakame adds texture to this dish. Substitute with wood ear fungus if you can't get your hands on it.

My love of scampi comes from working at Tetsuya's. My first section at Tet's was prepping his iconic dish of sashimi with foie gras and walnut oil. It remains one of the most amazing dishes I've ever eaten. Raw scampi is at once creamy and sweet. In fact, it's one of the sweetest shellfish you can eat. Australians are also fortunate that Tasmania has some of the best uni in the world. I wanted to combine the scampi with uni, which – aside from my wife – is one of the greatest loves of my life. I wanted to pair it with Vietnamese flavours because I don't know any raw fish dishes in the cuisine of my heritage. In a way, this dish is super simple: take lots of Vietnamese flavours, mix it up with great raw seafood and serve it.

CEVICHE of SCAMPI and SEA URCHIN with VIETNAMESE FLAVOURS

Serves 4

DRESSING

250 ml (9 fl oz/1 cup) nuoc cham (Essentials, page 244)
2 tablespoons fish sauce
1 tablespoon lime juice
2 teaspoons ót tương (Essentials, page 244)
1 tablespoon finely grated ginger

Whisk all the ingredients together in a bowl until well combined. Unused dressing will keep in a jar in the fridge for up to 2 weeks.

SCAMPI AND UNI

8 large sashimi-grade scampi (langoustine)
80 g (2¾ oz) sashimi-grade uni (sea urchin roe)
shellfish oil (Essentials, page 237)
15 small Vietnamese baby coriander (cilantro) leaves
15 small shiso leaves
15 small Vietnamese mint leaves
1 lemongrass stem, pale part only, very thinly sliced
2 bird's eye chillies, very thinly sliced
2 tablespoons fried shallots (Essentials, page 242), to garnish

Pull the heads off the scampi and discard. Use a sharp serrated knife to cut down the middle of the tails lengthways, through the shell. Remove the digestive tracts and discard. Remove the meat from the shell.

In a bowl, evenly lay the scampi tails and sea urchin roe in a single layer with no overlapping. Spoon a few tablespoons of the dressing over the top and follow with a few drops of shellfish oil. Top with the fresh herbs, lemongrass and chillies. Finally, garnish with the fried shallots. Serve immediately.

HONG HACK
No time to deep-fry shallots or make nuoc cham? Buy them from your local Asian grocery store.

Thai beef salad is one of my favourite salads. I wanted to make an elegant version of this dish at Lotus, so this is my interpretation of the classic. There are no tricks here, but as with sashimi or any meat you eat raw, this recipe relies on using the best-quality beef you can afford; it makes all the difference.

CARPACCIO OF BEEF with THAI FLAVOURS

Serves 4

ROASTED RICE
4 tablespoons jasmine rice

Heat a small frying pan over a high heat and add the rice. Constantly move the pan and toss the rice to evenly toast the rice. Keep going until the rice turns dark brown and starts to smell really nutty – it should be on the verge of being burnt (but not quite). Transfer the rice to a mortar and use a pestle to grind it to a fine powder. Store in an airtight container.

FOR THE BEEF
400 g (14 oz) piece good-quality beef fillet
sea salt flakes
vegetable oil, for rubbing

Season the beef with salt and rub it evenly with oil. Heat a frying pan over a very high heat and, when the pan is hot, sear the beef until well browned on all sides. This should take no longer than 45 seconds, as you still want the meat to be raw inside. Transfer the beef to a plate and refrigerate for 30 minutes to firm up.

DRESSING
100 ml (3½ fl oz) freshly squeezed lime juice
2½ tablespoons fish sauce
2 bird's eye chillies, finely chopped
1 garlic clove, finely grated
100 ml (3½ fl oz) vegetable oil

Whisk all the ingredients together in a bowl and set aside.

GARNISH
2 spring onions (scallions), thinly sliced
15 leaves round leaf mint, finely chopped
15 leaves Thai basil, finely chopped
20 leaves coriander (cilantro), finely chopped
4 leaves sawtooth coriander (cilantro), thinly sliced
1 lemongrass stem, pale part only, very thinly sliced
4 kaffir lime leaves, very thinly sliced

TO SERVE

Cut the piece of beef into roughly 3 mm (⅛ inch) thick slices against the grain, which gives it a better mouthfeel. Distribute the beef evenly among four plates, trying not to overlap the slices too much. Season each slice with a few sea salt flakes, then whisk the dressing and spoon a little over each slice of meat. Garnish with the spring onions, herbs, lemongrass and lime leaves, making sure each slice of beef is covered. Finish with a sprinkling of roasted rice.

This was a classic entrée at Lotus and one of the simplest. In my opinion, pork belly and watermelon is a perfect combination. The freshness and juiciness of the melon works well to cut the fatty richness of the pork belly. Add the bitterness of witlof, and it balances out the sweetness of the melon and sherry caramel.

PORK BELLY with WATERMELON, WITLOF and SHERRY CARAMEL

Serves 6 as an entrée

1 kg (2 lb 4 oz) piece pork belly
5 litres (175 fl oz/20 cups) Chinese masterstock (Essentials, page 234)

To prepare the pork belly, follow the braised pork belly method (page 54).

When cold and pressed, cut the pork belly into 2 cm (¾ inch) cubes, allowing for 3–4 cubes per person. You may have some left over, but that's not such a bad thing.

SHERRY VINEGAR CARAMEL

210 g (7½ oz) caster (superfine) sugar
½ teaspoon salt
2 tablespoons sherry vinegar

Put a small plate in the freezer. Add the sugar, salt and 2½ tablespoons water to a small saucepan over a high heat. Resist the urge to stir as the sugar melts. When the mixture starts to caramelise (about 185°C/365°F on a sugar thermometer), carefully pour in the sherry vinegar. If the mixture is too thin, bring it back to the boil, as it may need a little reducing. To test if the caramel is done, remove the plate from the freezer and spoon a small amount of the caramel onto it. After some seconds, the caramel should become the consistency of honey.

YOU WILL ALSO NEED

½ seedless watermelon, flesh only
1 witlof (chicory)
vegetable oil, for deep-frying
juice of 1 lemon
extra virgin olive oil, to dress

TO SERVE

Slice the watermelon into 1 cm (½ inch) pieces. Cut these into isosceles, or long triangles. Separate the witlof into individual leaves. Wash them and halve each lengthways.

Fill a large heavy-based saucepan or deep-fryer one-third full with oil and heat to 180°C (350°F) or until a cube of bread dropped into the oil turns golden in 15 seconds. Deep-fry the pork belly cubes in batches for about 4 minutes until golden, caramelised and crisp. Drain on paper towels then put all the pieces in a bowl. Spoon a few tablespoons of sherry caramel over the top and give it a stir to ensure the pieces are evenly coated.

Divide the pieces of pork among six plates. Dress the watermelon slices with a little lemon juice and lean a few pieces up against the pork. Dress the witlof leaves in a little lemon juice, olive oil and salt and arrange a few of these around the plates. Serve it up.

I was first introduced to black pudding at Pello. It's the kind of Franglo thing that chefs such as Marco Pierre White champion and it is often paired with scallops. When I started working at Marque Restaurant in Sydney, I finally learnt how to make it properly. It was both a nightmare and a bloodbath. We had to poach it lightly in a big pot of water at a constant 82°C (180°F). The first time I had to make it I thought: 'Why do I have to go through this much trouble to cook this?' Then I ate it and was completely converted. This version is really creamy and soft and when you pan-fry it, you get that crispy exterior and the softness on the inside. This recipe is a culmination of the techniques I learnt at Marque and Bentley Restaurant + Bar, but also contains my own flourishes. There are heaps of ways to serve it, but it pairs particularly well with shellfish or squid.

BLACK PUDDING

Makes a shitload

2 litres (70 fl oz/8 cups) pig's blood
grapeseed oil, for frying
6 large onions, finely chopped
20 garlic cloves, finely chopped
1¾ tablespoons fine salt
2 tablespoons smoked paprika
1 tablespoon Chinese five-spice
1 tablespoon ground star anise
1 tablespoon ground allspice
1 teaspoon ground cinnamon
1 teaspoon ground cloves
250 ml (9 fl oz/1 cup) cooking sake
250 ml (9 fl oz/1 cup) Shaoxing wine
250 ml (9 fl oz/1 cup) thin (pouring) cream
1 kg (2 lb 4 oz) pork back fat, in 5 mm (¼ inch) dice
200 g (7 oz) dry breadcrumbs
150 g (5½ oz) egg yolks

Heat a little oil in a large frying pan over a medium heat. Add the onions and garlic with the salt and spices and cook for about 5 minutes or until everything is softened. Turn the heat up to high and add the sake and Shaoxing wine. Keep simmering until the liquid has reduced by half.

Add the cream and again reduce by half. Add the back fat and breadcrumbs and mix them in well with a spoon (it should thicken quite a lot because of the breadcrumbs). Remove from the pan and transfer to a bowl to cool slightly.

Meanwhile use a hand-held blender to combine the pig's blood and egg yolks. This helps to get rid of any blood clots and to achieve a smooth texture.

Once the mixture is nice and smooth, add it to the creamy onions and combine well.

Preheat the oven to 80°C (175°F/Gas ⅓). Line a couple of shallow roasting tins with baking paper. Divide the pudding mixture between the trays then cover them really tightly with plastic wrap. In the restaurant, we'd put these in a combination steam oven. At home, you can use a water bath technique, similar to the method for baking custards.

Put each sealed dish into a larger, deeper one. Fill the larger one with water to halfway up the sides of the smaller one. Put these in the oven and bake for 1¼ hours. Remove the pudding tins from their water baths and refrigerate, which will help to firm the puddings. Once cool, un-mould the trays and cut the pudding into your desired sizes and shapes. They're best served pan-fried immediately prior to serving, to crisp up the outside.

HONG HACK
Using a skewer or meat thermometer, do what you do to check if a cake is done. If the skewer comes out (mostly) clean, you're good to go.

Make sure you blitz the blood to remove any clots before pouring.

Mix the blood and the bread mixture really thoroughly.

Lining the trays with baking paper is a must.

BLACK PUDDING SERVING SUGGESTIONS

- Pan-fried with a fried egg on toast
- Pan-fried and served in a banh mi with all the trimmings
- Wrapped up in a spring roll and deep-fried
- Fried and served with some grilled seafood and nuoc cham gel (Essentials, page 244)
- Combine black pudding with prawns in a wonton and poach in supreme stock (Essentials, page 235)
- Crumb it, fry it and serve it in a taco
- Blend it into red meat jus to add an extra dimension of flavour
- Serve it cold as part of a charcuterie platter with crusty bread

This dish was influenced by my time working with Brent Savage at Bentley Restaurant and Bar. At the time, we were completely into what the Spanish chefs were doing: taking classic Spanish flavours and presenting them in a modern way. Black pudding and calamari is a match made in heaven. The rich intense creaminess of the black pudding really goes well with the sweet flavour and texture of calamari. It's the ultimate surf and turf combination.

BLACK PUDDING with CALAMARI, ROMESCO SALSA and SAUCE NERO

Serves 4

black pudding (recipe, page 26)
vegetable oil, for frying

Prepare the black pudding following the recipe instructions, but halving the quantities. Cut it into twelve 2 cm (¾ inch) cubes.

ROMESCO SALSA

1 red capsicum (pepper)
3 roma (plum) tomatoes, seeded and finely diced
3 tablespoons toasted flaked almonds, crushed
1 small red Asian shallot, finely chopped
½ teaspoon finely grated garlic
15 parsley leaves, finely chopped
3 tablespoons extra virgin olive oil
1 tablespoon sherry vinegar
1 teaspoon caster (superfine) sugar

Roast the capsicum over an open flame such as a gas hob or barbecue until the skin is nicely charred all over. When the skin has blackened, immediately remove from the heat and transfer to a bowl, then cover with plastic wrap, which will loosen the skin with steam.

After 20 minutes or so, when the capsicum is cool enough to touch, use your fingers to gently remove the skin and seeds. Finely dice the flesh, then transfer to a bowl. Add the rest of the salsa ingredients, season to taste and mix well. Refrigerate until ready to serve.

PARSLEY OIL

1 bunch of flat-leaf (Italian) parsley, roughly chopped including stems
250 ml (9 fl oz/1 cup) grapeseed oil

Put the parsley and oil in a blender and whizz on a high speed for about 2 minutes, or until you get a very fine purée. Store the parsley oil in a sterilised jar in the fridge until needed.

SAUCE NERO

1 tablespoon cuttlefish ink
100 ml (3½ fl oz) chicken stock (Essentials, page 236)
1 tablespoon shellfish oil (Essentials, page 237)
2 teaspoons lemon juice

Heat all the ingredients in a small saucepan over a high heat and whisk until well combined. Bring to the boil, then reduce the heat to medium–low and simmer the sauce for 5 minutes. Set aside in a warm place.

CALAMARI
1 whole large calamari, cleaned
1 tablespoon vegetable oil

Cut the calamari into 2 cm (¾ inch) wide strips.
Add the oil to a non-stick frying pan over a very high
heat. Season the calamari strips with salt and, when
the oil starts to smoke, add the strips skin-side down,
and throw in the legs as well.

After about 25 seconds, flip the calamari pieces
over. Turn the heat off and leave the calamari to fry
for another 25–30 seconds.

The pan has to be hot, and the process must
be quick so you don't overcook the calamari, which
will render it rubbery. Remove from the pan and
keep warm.

TO SERVE

Add some oil to a non-stick frying pan over a high
heat and, when the oil starts to smoke, carefully add
the black pudding pieces. Don't touch the black
pudding for about 2 minutes, just enjoy watching
it fry and caramelise. When a crust has developed
on the bottom of the pan, use a spatula to carefully
flip the pieces and fry the other side for a further
2 minutes.

Put 3 pieces of black pudding on each of
four plates. Add a few pieces of calamari, then
spoon 3 tablespoons of the romesco salsa around
the plate. To finish, spoon on some parsley oil and
sauce nero.

HONG HACK
See the salt and pepper squid
recipe (page 165) for tips on
how to clean calamari, or ask
your fishmonger.

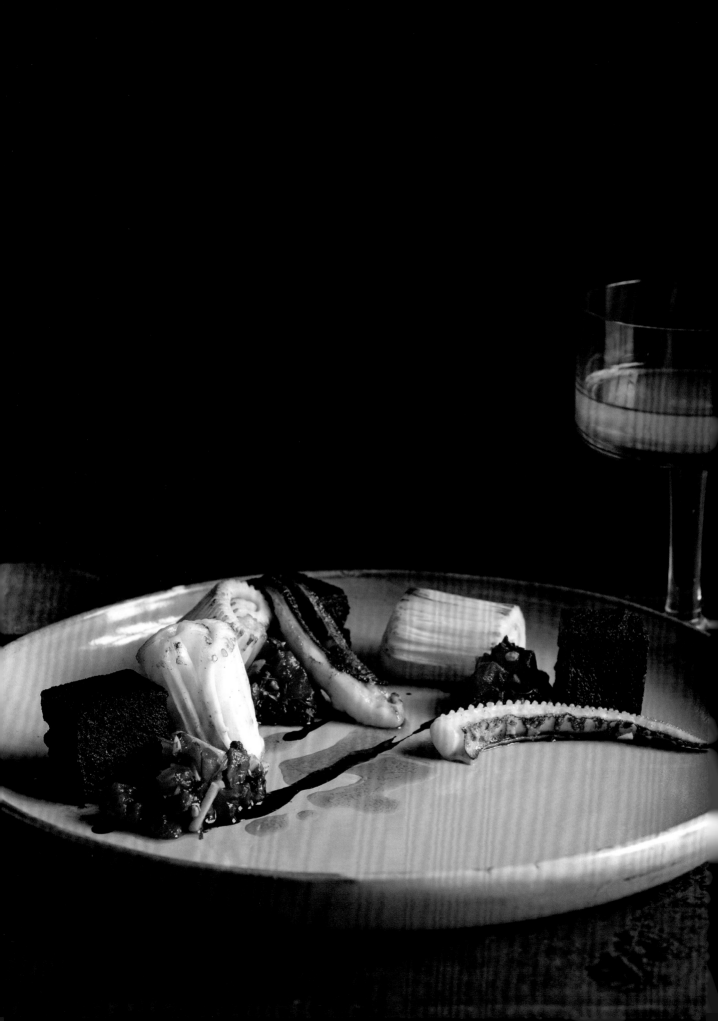

This is a really clean, simple dish that originated from my opening menu at Lotus. Any firm white-fleshed fish can be used – snapper, bar cod or coral trout works well. When I created this, I wanted to make an Asian-inspired dish that could be eaten as a stand-alone main course. It's basically a noodle soup with a piece of fish on top. A nage is a flavourful broth used to poach meat in. You can use this nage recipe to poach fish or chicken, or thicken it into a sauce. Start this recipe a day ahead.

STEAMED FISH with FUNGI, SNOW PEA SPROUTS, CAPELLINI and GINGER NAGE

Serves 4

DAY 1

GINGER VEGETABLE NAGE
5 carrots, peeled, thinly sliced
2 large celery stalks, thinly sliced
2 large brown onions, thinly sliced
3 garlic cloves, thinly sliced
1 bay leaf
10 cm (4 inch) piece ginger, thinly sliced
½ lemon, skin on, thinly sliced
4 coriander (cilantro) roots, cleaned, finely chopped
4 thyme sprigs
150 ml (5 fl oz) white wine
125 ml (4 fl oz/½ cup) shiro-dashi
2 tablespoons white soy sauce
2 tablespoons kombu extract (optional)
about 1 tablespoon salt
about 4 tablespoons raw sugar

Add the carrots, celery, onions, garlic, bay leaf and ginger to a large saucepan and fill with enough water to cover the ingredients. Bring to the boil over a high heat and simmer for 5 minutes.

Add the lemon, coriander roots, thyme and wine and turn off the heat. Transfer the contents of the pan to a large plastic container and cover immediately with a tight-fitting lid. Put the container in the fridge for 24 hours to enable the flavours to infuse.

DAY 2

Strain the solids out and pour the liquid (you should have about 2 litres/70 fl oz/8 cups) into a large saucepan. Bring to the boil and add the shiro-dashi, white soy sauce and the kombu extract, if using.

Add the salt and sugar, to taste. It should taste really umami with some sweetness and a little fishiness from the dashi and it should be super tasty, on the border of over-seasoned but not. Remove from the heat and cool a little, then refrigerate until ready to serve.

120 g (4¼ oz) dried capellini (angel hair pasta)
4 x 200 g (7 oz) skinless fillets of firm white-fleshed fish (such as snapper, coral trout)
vegetable oil, for frying
150 g (5½ oz) fresh enoki mushrooms, separated into thin clusters
100 g (3½ oz) fresh wood-ear mushrooms
100 g (3½ oz) snow pea (mangetout) sprouts, bottom half discarded
2 spring onions (scallions), thinly sliced
2 tablespoons ginger oil (Essentials, page 238)
baby coriander (cilantro) leaves, to garnish

Bring a large saucepan of salted water to the boil. Add the pasta and cook until al dente, according to packet instructions. Drain, refresh the pasta under cold water and set aside.

Season the fish fillets and transfer to a plate inside a large steamer over a saucepan of simmering water. Cook for 5–7 minutes over low–medium heat, depending on how thick the fillets are.

To test if the fish is done, insert a skewer into the thickest part of the fillet. If it pulls out easily, the fish is ready. Once done, remove from the heat, set aside and cover to keep warm.

Meanwhile, heat a large frying pan or wok over a high heat and add a little vegetable oil. Reduce the heat to medium and add the mushrooms and snow pea sprouts. Cook, stirring continuously, for about 2 minutes. Season with salt and then, when the vegetables are nearly done, add the pasta. Mix thoroughly.

TO FINISH

Divide the mixture between four bowls and place a steamed fish fillet on top of each.

Bring the nage to the boil in a small saucepan and then remove from the heat.

TO SERVE

Add the spring onions and pour the nage over and around the fish. Spoon ginger oil over the top and garnish with baby coriander leaves. Serve immediately.

Chawanmushi is a Japanese savoury steamed egg custard that, when made well, is possibly one of my favourite things to eat. Whenever it's on the menu at a Japanese restaurant, I have to order it just to see how good it is. If it comes out lukewarm, then it wasn't made fresh to order. This dish should be served super hot, and should tremble like panna cotta when you put a spoon through it. My version pays homage to Tetsuya Wakuda and my time spent at Tetsuya's – spanner crab and shellfish oil always remind me of those days.

CHAWANMUSHI, SPANNER CRAB and SHELLFISH OIL

Serves 4 as a small entrée

CHAWANMUSHI

2½ tablespoons thin (pouring) cream
3¾ tablespoons shiro-dashi
3 eggs

Whisk all the ingredients together with 350 ml (12 fl oz) water in a bowl and strain through a fine sieve into a jug. Divide among four small bowls and cover each bowl very tightly with plastic wrap. Put the bowls in a large steamer and place over a saucepan of simmering water for 6–8 minutes or until set. They should be quite firm with a little wobble in the centre.

VEGETABLE NAGE GLAZE

200 ml (7 fl oz) seasoned ginger vegetable nage (recipe, page 32)
1 tablespoon potato starch mixed with a little water to form a slurry

Bring the vegetable nage to the boil in a small saucepan. Start to gradually whisk in the slurry and continue whisking and adding slurry until the nage thickens. You will not need to add all the slurry, just keep going until you achieve a thick sauce without any lumps.

THE REST

120 g (4¼ oz) cooked crabmeat
1 tablespoon trout roe, to garnish
chopped chives, to garnish
1–2 teaspoons shellfish oil (Essentials, page 237)

Put the crabmeat in a bowl and place in a bamboo steamer over a saucepan of simmering water for 30 seconds, or long enough to heat it through.

TO SERVE

When the bowls of chawanmushi are cooked, remove the plastic wrap and divide the crabmeat among the four bowls. Spoon the hot vegetable nage glaze on top, making sure you cover the whole surface area of the chawanmushi. Garnish each with a teaspoon of trout roe, some chopped chives and a few drops of shellfish oil.

HONG HACK
Depending on your set-up at home, you can use anything from a ramekin to a wide, shallow bowl to steam your chawanmushi. Make sure whatever you choose fits inside your steamer basket comfortably with the bamboo lid on.

This was the most popular side dish at Lotus and it has a bit of a story to it. When I was working at Bentley Restaurant + Bar, the pastry chef at the time, Dave Verheul, would always make this zucchini, crouton and parmesan salad for the staff meal. It was so delicious that when I went to Lotus, I decided to put it on as a side dish. Diners would ask: 'Who is Dave?' Sometimes the waiters would tell them Dave was the dishwasher, or the apprentice at Lotus, and one time we even had to send out a guy from the kitchen pretending to be Dave, because a customer loved it so much they wanted to meet him. After a few months I found out that it wasn't even Dave's salad. It belonged to Alex Herbert, who had a bistro called Bird Cow Fish. Dave had worked there before moving to the Bentley and had brought it with him. It is a fantastic accompaniment to any roast or barbecued meat or fish dish. Thanks Dave (and Alex).

DAVE'S ZUCCHINI SALAD

Serves 4 as a side salad

CROUTONS
400 g (14 oz) piece of bread (preferably sourdough), crusts removed
extra virgin olive oil, for coating

Preheat the oven to 150°C (300°F/Gas 2). Tear the bread into small bite-sized pieces and spread them on a baking tray. Toss them liberally in oil and season with salt and pepper. Bake in the oven until golden and crisp.

LEMON VINAIGRETTE
100 ml (3½ fl oz) lemon juice
350 ml (12 fl oz) extra virgin olive oil

Whisk the ingredients together in a bowl, and be sure to whisk again immediately prior to dressing the salad.

ZUCCHINI
4 medium zucchini (courgettes), both yellow and green is preferable
1 bunch flat-leaf (Italian) parsley, leaves only
100 g (3½ oz) parmesan cheese
sea salt flakes

Using a mandolin, shave the zucchini as thinly as possible into small rounds and put them in a bowl along with the croutons and the parsley leaves. Finely grate three-quarters of the parmesan into the salad and generously dress with the vinaigrette. Season generously with sea salt flakes and freshly ground black pepper and toss well. Transfer the salad to a serving bowl and grate the rest of the cheese over the top before serving.

HONG HACK
Parmesan is a hard Italian cheese with a lot of flavour and a bit of bite. You can substitute another hard Italian-style cheese.

The myths that surround this burger are hilarious. I mostly have my mates (mainly chefs and massive pigs) to thank for hyping it up. In 2008, I was named Josephine Pignolet Best Young Chef at the *SMH Good Food Guide Awards*. The award is a scholarship grant given to encourage chefs to travel and stage (culinary unpaid internship) overseas anywhere that inspires them. I decided to head to New York for eight weeks to wd~50, one of the city's most celebrated restaurants run by chef and icon, Wylie Dufresne.

When I arrived in NYC, I came to realise I didn't really know what a good burger was. So JJ, wd~50's prep chef (and now sous chef) became my burger spirit guide. Every night, after work, he would take me to different burger places. When I asked him where to go for a good burger, he'd reply with questions like: 'Do you prefer a really greasy burger? Do you like a thick patty? Would you want a steamed bun? Do you like really sloppy burgers?' JJ seemed to know of every kind of burger in existence in the Big Apple.

Thanks to JJ, I really like burgers. Shake Shack is probably one of my favourites. The bun is super soft, and they ask you how you want your patty cooked. They use great quality beef, so I always ask for it medium–rare or rare if the patty is really thin. That aroma that hits you when you join the queues snaking out the door of the Madison Square Park mothership... you can almost taste the juicy beef straight off the grill... it's enough to make you cartoon-float to the front of the queue.

THIS IS THE ANATOMY OF MY PERFECT BURGER

{WHICH BECAME KNOWN AS THE LOTUS BURGER}

THE BUN

It starts with a steamed bun. Like a McDonald's steamed bun, the kind they use for their Filet-o-Fish. There's an unwritten code that chefs have regarding McDonald's. You go there, and you custom-order a burger using the best elements. Basically, we want to recreate a double cheeseburger with Big Mac sauce on a steamed bun with bacon, but better.

A crucial element of that burger is the steamed bun. A great burger should be squished, so that's where we started. I like to steam a Tip Top bun.

HEINZ TOMATO KETCHUP

The only ketchup you should be using. Burger purists would consider it to be sacrilege to use any other brand.

PICKLES

These add acidity and texture. Store-bought ones are fine – look for big dill gherkins, slice them thinly and put them on top just before the bun goes on.

BACON, CHARGRILLED

I use a brand called Schulz, from South Australia. I like it because it's not too salty and there's a good amount of fat and smokiness to it. You want it to be streaky (belly) bacon.

Because the patty is grilled in a pan, rather than on a flame grill, the way you cook the bacon is the key element in getting that chargrilled flavour into the burger. You want it to develop a few grill marks, but not be too well done. Like the patty, it should be a bit juicy.

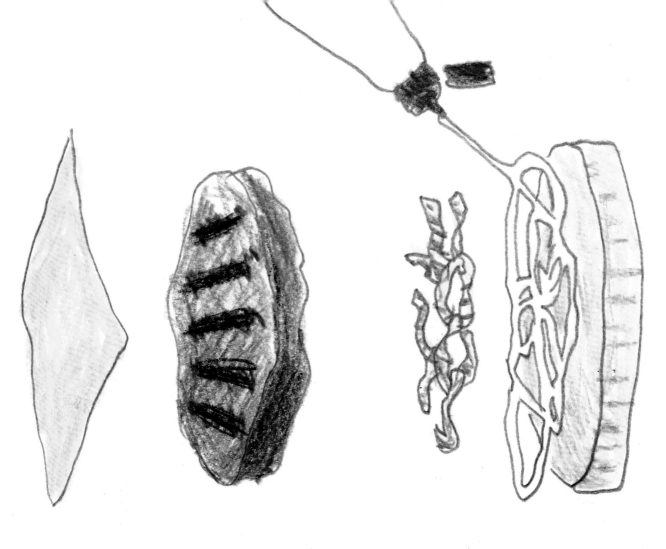

CHEESE

Selection is crucial. American cheese is preferable – that bright yellow stuff that's not really cheese – but a processed Australian cheddar also works well.

THE PATTY

We knew we wanted to mince our own meat in house at Lotus. As with places like Shake Shack, Minetta Tavern and almost all great NYC burger joints, they have their own custom blend of beef cuts.

We played with nearly every combination and cut we could think of. It had to be juicy, so a lot of time went into experimenting with the meat-to-fat content. Patty experimentation started with a mixture of short rib, brisket and chuck, with regular beef fat. Then one day, our butcher heard what we were trying to do, and suggested we use the dry-aged beef fat he normally threw away as offcuts. We couldn't believe they would throw away something so perfectly good, so we took it and used it.

After extensive testing, it comes down to this: 80 per cent beef, 20 per cent dry-aged beef fat. That's it. No seasonings, flavours or binders, Worcestershire sauce, breadcrumbs, herbs, soy, nothing. To do so, would be to go down the track of creating another Australian institution: the rissole. In and of itself, that's not a bad thing, but in a burger you're heading down the wrong path.

As chefs, we're taught to season at every stage of the cooking process, but it's a different story with hamburgers. Salt draws out moisture and fat, so when you cook it, the proteins set really hard, which is not the way to create a really juicy patty.

We have American chef and respected mega molecular gastronomic geek Dave Arnold, founder of the Museum of Food and Drink, to thank for the realisation that salt is, in fact, the enemy in this recipe. The only time the beef sees salt is just before it hits the pan to be cooked.

CARAMELISED ONIONS

These add a depth of flavour and sweetness. At the end of the caramelisation process, we add brown miso paste to the onions, which also ups the umami. I can't remember whether I learned about this in Bon Appétit magazine or Food & Wine, but it just goes to show that reading anything and everything about cooking pays off – this tip is gold.

JAPANESE MAYO

We like it because it has that certain level of umami that others don't have (read: it contains MSG). Japanese mayo is also the perfect consistency for burgers. It's creamy and it's neither too solid nor too liquid. And most importantly, it's not salad cream, which a lot of Australians mistakenly believe is mayo. It's not.

To make this recipe properly, you will need a mincer attachment for your food processor. If you don't have one, you can ask your butcher to help you out.

LOTUS CHEESEBURGER

Serves 5

THE PATTIES
400 g (14 oz) grain-fed beef brisket, top layer of fat removed
400 g (14 oz) grain-fed beef chuck, excess fat removed
200 g (7 oz) dry-aged beef fat

THE CARAMELISED ONIONS
50 g (1¾ oz) unsalted butter
3 large white onions, thinly sliced
1 tablespoon brown miso

THE REST
1 tablespoon vegetable oil
5 slices of American-style processed cheddar cheese
10 smoked bacon slices, about 10 cm (4 inches) in length
5 soft sesame seed hamburger buns, 13 cm (5 inches) in diameter
Japanese mayonnaise (Kenko brand)
3 large gherkins (pickles), sliced on a mandolin to 2 mm (¹⁄₁₆ inch) thick
Heinz Tomato Ketchup

For the patties, slice the brisket and beef chuck into nice long pieces that will fit inside the mincer. Transfer the slices to a bowl and put in the freezer for about 1 hour, or until the meat has just started to firm up. This will prevent the meat and fat from getting too hot and melting when going through the mincer. Carefully feed the meat through the mincer, making sure to alternate pieces of brisket, chuck and fat.

Put the mix in the fridge to firm up for 1 hour. Moisten your hands with a little vegetable oil, divide the mixture into about 5 x 140 g (5 oz) patties and flatten them out evenly between your hands. Make sure each patty is about 5 mm (¼ inch) wider than the diameter of the bun because they shrink when cooked.

For the caramelised onions, melt the butter in a shallow saucepan over a medium heat, then add the onions and a pinch of salt. Cook over a medium heat, stirring continuously until the onions have softened and cooked down to a dark brown colour.

Add the miso paste and gently stir it through until well combined. Transfer to a container and keep warm.

Preheat a chargrill/grill plate to high for the bacon. Preheat the oven to 180°C (350°F/Gas 4). Meanwhile, to prepare the hamburger buns, place a bamboo steamer on top of a saucepan of simmering water over a medium–low heat.

To cook the patties, add a little oil to a large frying pan over a high heat. When the oil starts to smoke, season the patties on both sides with a little salt and place gently in the pan. Fry for about 2 minutes on one side and then flip. Cook the second side for 30 seconds. The patty should develop a nice brown crust.

Top each patty with two slices of cheese, cover the pan with a lid and leave for 1 minute on the heat, which will melt the cheese. While the patties are steaming, grill the bacon on both sides until nicely charred, but not crispy. Soften the hamburger buns in the bamboo steamer for about 30 seconds.

To assemble the burgers, put a tablespoon of Japanese mayonnaise on the bottom half of a bun, smoothing it out evenly with the back of a spoon so it covers the entire base. Spread with an even layer of caramelised onions, then add a cooked patty, cheese side up.

Arrange two slices of bacon side by side on top of the cheese, then place the gherkin slices on top in a single layer that covers all areas of the patty. Finally, top the patty with ketchup, starting from the middle and moving in a spiral direction working towards the outside. Finish by putting the bun top on top. That's it.

HONG HACK
This recipe may yield a few more patties than you need. That's probably not such a bad thing.

I hate sarsaparilla (or root beer as the Americans call it). I find the aniseed medicinal flavour to be a bit gross, as it sort of reminds me of a non-alcoholic Jägermeister... so what's the point? Here's the BUT: using it as a braising liquid really works! Those exact flavours I dislike as a drink give this sauce a beautiful depth when it is reduced. Although I don't really subscribe to the whole 'three-course meal' style of dining anymore, this was one of the most popular mains on the Lotus menu, and it encapsulates that 'East meets West' philosophy beautifully.

BEEF CHEEKS BRAISED in SARSAPARILLA, CARROT and ORANGE, XO CRUMBS

Serves 4

BRAISING LIQUID
vegetable oil, for frying
2 brown onions, roughly chopped
4 tablespoons roughly chopped fresh ginger
6 garlic cloves, lightly crushed
1.5 litres (52 fl oz/6 cups) sarsaparilla
8 star anise
2 cinnamon sticks
150 ml (5 fl oz) light soy sauce
500 ml (17 fl oz/2 cups) chicken stock (Essentials, page 236)
2½ tablespoons balsamic vinegar

Add some oil to an ovenproof braising saucepan and heat over a high heat. Fry the onions, ginger and garlic until caramelised and slightly burnt. Pour in the sarsaparilla to deglaze the saucepan. Add the remaining ingredients, bring to the boil and simmer for about 20 minutes to develop the flavours.

BEEF CHEEKS
4 large (250 g/9 oz each) beef cheeks, trimmed of all outer sinew and fat
vegetable oil, for frying

Preheat the oven to 180°C (350°F/Gas 4). Season the beef cheeks liberally with salt and set aside for 30 minutes.

Heat a large frying pan over a high heat and add some oil. When it is hot, sear the cheeks, turning them until nicely browned on both sides.

Transfer the cheeks to the braising liquid, cover the surface with baking paper and then secure with a tight-fitting lid. When the braised beef cheeks have been brought back to the boil, remove from the heat and transfer the saucepan to the oven for 4–5 hours.

Set a timer and, about halfway through the cooking time, turn the cheeks and ensure there's enough liquid to stop them drying out. If not, add a little water. The end result: the cheeks should be soft enough to eat with a spoon.

Remove the pan from the oven and allow the cheeks to rest in the braising liquid for about 2 hours. This will allow them to absorb more of the liquid. After that time has passed, carefully transfer the cheeks to a plate and quickly cover them with plastic wrap to prevent them drying out.

Strain the braising liquid into another saucepan, heat over a high heat, and then reduce the liquid to a light sauce consistency. Don't reduce it too much at this stage, as you'll finish it off closer to serving. Remove from the heat, cover and set aside.

XO CRUMBS

300 g (10½ oz) 2-day-old sourdough bread, crust removed, cut into smallish cubes
100 ml (3½ fl oz) extra virgin olive oil
4 tablespoons XO sauce (Essentials, page 239)

Put the sourdough bread into the bowl of a food processor and whizz until coarse crumbs form. Spread the breadcrumbs on a tray and leave in a warm place (or the oven at a very low temperature) for a few hours to dehydrate. Once the crumbs are firm and have lost all of their moisture, they are ready to cook.

Put a large frying pan over a medium heat and heat the oil. Add the XO sauce and fry for 20 seconds, or until it becomes aromatic. Add the breadcrumbs and mix thoroughly with a wooden spoon so the crumbs soak up the oil evenly. Turn the heat down to low and continue frying the crumbs, stirring constantly, until they are light golden in colour. Season with salt and pepper, then drain on paper towels. Allow to cool.

CARROT AND ORANGE PURÉE

4 large carrots, very thinly sliced
1 large orange, zested and juiced

Put the carrots in a small saucepan and cover with water. Add a pinch of salt and bring to the boil. Cover the pan and cook the carrots over a medium heat until they are very tender. Test this by taking a slice and placing it between your thumb and index finger. If it squishes easily, it's ready. By the time the carrots are ready, most of the water should have evaporated.

Drain the carrots and put them in a blender with the orange zest and about 2½ tablespoons of orange juice. Purée, then season to taste with a little salt and set aside.

TO SERVE

1 bunch curly kale, leaves only

Blanch the kale leaves in salted boiling water for 1 minute. Drain, refresh in cold water and set aside.

Arrange the beef cheeks in a single layer in a large shallow saucepan or frying pan. Add the braising liquid and bring to the boil. Cover with a lid, reduce the heat to medium and heat the cheeks through, basting every now and then with the simmering sauce. Continue to cook until the beef cheeks are heated through (you can check by inserting a knife or a metal skewer into the centre; if the skewer is hot, the meat is done). Remove the lid, turn up the heat and continue to baste the cheeks until they look nicely glazed and the sauce has reduced and thickened.

Reheat the carrot purée and spoon some on each of four serving plates. Add a glazed beef cheek to each plate, some reduced sauce and a few kale leaves. Finally, spoon or press some XO crumbs over the cheeks and serve at once.

HONG HACKS

If you don't have an ovenproof braising pan you can carefully transfer the braising liquid and beef cheeks (after they have been brought to the boil on the stove) into a roasting tin that has been lined with baking paper. Seal the tray with a few layers of foil and continue with the directions.

XO crumbs will keep in an airtight container in the fridge for up to 2 weeks. Any leftover crumbs will work well as a crunchy topping for all sorts of dishes.

This dish became my signature dessert when I was at Lotus and it had a loyal and devoted following. At the time, everyone in Sydney was trying really hard to do something molecular and Alex Stupak-esque with desserts. While I admired the American chef's inventive creations, I wanted to do something fun and tasty with real texture, and something my customers could relate to.

LOTUS ICE CREAM SUNDAE with RASPBERRIES and HONEYCOMB

Serves 6

CHOCOLATE FUDGE
340 g (11¾ oz) caster (superfine) sugar
70 g (2½ oz) liquid glucose
35 g (1¼ oz) cocoa powder
325 g (11½ oz) dark chocolate, cut into small pieces
75 g (2½ oz) unsalted butter
15 g (½ oz) xanthan gum

Fill a large saucepan with 390 ml (13½ fl oz) water. Add the sugar, glucose, cocoa powder and 1 teaspoon salt and heat over a high heat. Bring to the boil, then add the chocolate and butter. Reduce the heat to a simmer and cook until the chocolate and butter melt. Whisk to combine and then bring back up to the boil. Using a hand-held blender, mix in the xanthan gum, which will thicken the fudge. Remove from the heat and allow to cool, then transfer the fudge into a covered container and put in the fridge, where it will keep for up to 2 weeks.

HONEYCOMB
170 g (5¾ oz) caster (superfine) sugar
1 tablespoon honey
65 g (2¼ oz) liquid glucose
2 teaspoons bicarbonate of soda (baking soda)

Line a small baking tray with baking paper. To make the caramel, add the sugar, honey, liquid glucose and 1½ tablespoons water to a small saucepan and put over a high heat. Resist the urge to stir, just allow the heat to begin to transform the sugar. If crystals start to appear, you can give the saucepan a little swirl, or use a wet pastry brush to brush down the side of the pan.

Once a light caramel is achieved (about 155°C/310°F on a sugar thermometer), quickly whisk in the bicarbonate of soda, then immediately pour the mixture onto the prepared tray. Leave to cool at room temperature until it hardens. Break the honeycomb into smaller pieces and store in an airtight container. Do not refrigerate, as the sugars will melt and soften the honeycomb.

RASPBERRY SAUCE
500 g (1 lb 2 oz/4 cups) frozen raspberries
175 g (6 oz) caster (superfine) sugar

Add the raspberries and sugar to a small saucepan and cook over a medium heat, stirring occasionally, for about 20 minutes or until a semi-thick consistency is achieved. You don't want to cook the sauce too long as this will create jam; there should still be a little freshness about it.

TO SERVE
Vanilla ice cream (recipe, page 194), or a good-quality vanilla bean ice cream will do you just fine
fresh raspberries
salted peanuts

Warm the chocolate fudge in a microwave until hot. Spoon some raspberry sauce into each of six serving bowls. Add 2 scoops of vanilla ice cream and top with some shards of honeycomb, raspberries and peanuts. Serve the chocolate fudge in a jug on the side so everyone can pour as little (or as much) as they like.

CHAPTER TWO

Ms G's

After our research trip to New York and the eventual evolution of the Lotus menu into being more reflective of me, it was time to start shaping Ms G's.

Ms G's combined the fine dining training Jow and I had undertaken with the food we liked to eat – junk food, food from our heritage and nostalgic food we loved eating as kids.

The other revelation for me at the time was that I didn't want to chase critical acclaim anymore. While I'd had some critical success with awards and solid reviews, I started to see a problem with how we are conditioned to associate success with critical acceptance. What proved a game-changer was when I finally had the realisation that true success was a consistently busy restaurant... and that awards are just a bonus (albeit a welcome one).

Around the same time we opened Ms G's, 'dude food' became 'a thing' in Sydney. Trends are tricky. On the one hand, they help chefs to track the evolution of good food and identify hot new ideas. On the other hand, as soon as one identifiable trend is replaced with another, it can spell trouble for the way your food is perceived. We're lucky at Ms G's because, despite the hype, the customers are loyal as the good food and great vibe will never be a passing fad. It's about tasty food made to share and a fun dining experience. I don't think it can get any more enduring or universal than that. Ms G's was a huge step up from the relatively small 50-seater Lotus. It's 100 seats over four levels, seven days a week. Although, at the time, it seemed insane to open such a vast, sprawling space, we were both committed and passionate.

DISHES
FROM THE
ORIGINAL
MS G'S
MENU

... these dishes still exist on the menu in some form.

MINI BANH MI

**VIETNAMESE
STEAK TARTARE**

STONER'S DELIGHT

CORN ON THE COB with **TOGARASHI SOUR CREAM, PARMESAN**

PRAWN TOAST with **YUZU AIOLI**

I love banh mi – it's food from my heritage and I wanted to put it on the menu. We decided to make Ms G's banh mi smaller so that diners could fit in other dishes as well. In my eyes, banh mi is up there with the most iconic sandwiches of the world. It's the perfect balance of richness, acidity, texture, freshness and spice. In short, everything you could ever want in a sandwich.

MINI PORK BANH MI

Serves 8

THE PORK
6 litres (210 fl oz/24 cups) Chinese masterstock (Essentials, page 234)
1.5 kg (3 lb 5 oz) pork belly, rib bones removed, skin on

Pour the masterstock into a stockpot and carefully add the pork belly. Bring to the boil. As soon as it's reached boiling point, turn the heat down and simmer for 3–4 hours or until the pork belly is tender.

Line a roasting tin (large enough to fit the pork belly) with baking paper. Carefully lift the pork belly from the stock, being mindful to keep everything in one piece (not easy to do, since the pork is very soft at this point).

Put the pork in the tin, skin side down. Cover with another piece of baking paper then a baking tray. Weight the tray with heavy objects such as tins of tomatoes then leave it overnight (unrefrigerated) to press the pork belly.

THE REST
1 loaf of chà lua (Vietnamese pork loaf)
vegetable oil, for frying
8 small, soft white rolls
pork liver pâté (Essentials, page 243)
6 salted cucumbers (Essentials, page 241)
pickled daikon and carrot (see Pickling liquid recipe, Essentials, page 241)
1 bunch coriander (cilantro), leaves only
Sriracha mayonnaise (Essentials, page 240)

Using a meat slicer or a very sharp knife, slice the chà lua as thinly as possible. Set aside. Cut the pork belly into pieces about 1.5 cm (⅝ inch) thick and about the same length as the rolls.

Fill a large heavy-based saucepan one-third full with oil and heat to 170°C (325°F) or until a cube of bread dropped into the oil turns golden in 20 seconds. Carefully drop in the pork belly pieces and fry until golden. Remove with a slotted spoon and drain on paper towel.

Cut the white rolls in half. Spread the bases generously with pork liver pâté. Top with a few slices of chà lua, then add the fried pork, followed in order by the salted cucumbers, pickled daikons and carrots, a few coriander leaves, and, finally, a generous dollop of Sriracha mayonnaise.

HONG HACK
This dish is meant to be fun and to be shared, so make it your own. If you're stuck for time, a side of roasted pork from your favourite Chinese BBQ restaurant will work fine.

GRILLED CORN with LIME and PARMESAN

Serves 4–6

SEASONED CREAM
500 g (1 lb 2 oz) Japanese mayonnaise
500 g (1 lb 2 oz) sour cream
1½ tablespoons ground cumin
3 tablespoons shichimi togarashi

Whisk all of the seasoned cream ingredients together in a bowl until combined. Set aside in the fridge.

6 cobs of corn, each one cut into three pieces
2 limes, halved
1 bunch coriander (cilantro), leaves only
100 g (3½ oz) wedge of parmesan, for grating

Steam or boil the pieces of corn until tender. Put on a hot chargrill pan or barbecue and cook, turning three or four times, until the kernels are a little bit charred. Remove from the grill and stab one end of each piece of corn with a short cocktail skewer that has little handles.

Liberally brush each piece of corn with the seasoned cream and arrange them on a platter. Squeeze some fresh lime juice over the top, making sure each piece of corn gets some. Scatter with coriander and then use a microplane to grate a liberal amount of parmesan over the top. Eat.

HONG HACK
If you can't get parmesan, substitute with any other hard parmesan-style cheese.

A dish influenced by one of my best friends, fellow chef, Louis Tikaram. Louis has a Fijian background and he once told me about one of Fiji's national dishes, called kokoda, which incorporates coconut milk into a ceviche mix. This is my take on kokoda (pronounced kokonda), which infuses some of my Vietnamese heritage into the dish. When I asked Louis what he thought about me doing that, he said: 'Sounds tasty.' And that's what the food at Ms G's is all about: tasty.

FIJIAN-STYLE SASHIMI of TREVALLY

Serves 2

DRESSING
80 ml (2½ fl oz/⅓ cup) nuoc cham (Essentials, page 244)
55 ml (1¾ fl oz) coconut cream
1 tablespoon ót tuóng (Essentials, page 244)
juice of ½ lime

Whisk all of the ingredients together in a bowl until well combined.

THE REST
200 g (7 oz) piece of sashimi-grade trevally, skinned and boned
1 small long red chilli, thinly sliced
4 cherry tomatoes, quartered
70 g (2½ oz) young coconut flesh, cut into thin strips
50 g (1¾ oz) salted cucumber (Essentials, page 241)
15 coriander (cilantro) leaves
1 red Asian shallot, thinly sliced

Slice the trevally into thin strips. Transfer the fish to a bowl with the remaining ingredients. Spoon about 100 ml (3½ fl oz) of the dressing over the fish and mix well. Don't worry if there looks like a lot of dressing, it starts to 'cook' the fish as you're eating it, which is how it's meant to be. Serve in bowls and enjoy immediately.

This is loosely based on a traditional Vietnamese dish where you wrap marinated lemongrass beef on a betel leaf, skewer it and grill it. It's called *bo la lot*. The classic pairing of beef and lemongrass is a real expression of the Vietnamese flavour profile. Using classic Viet herbs completes the dish by adding freshness. The dressing is almost Thai, in the way that it's about two levels up in flavour punch than your average Vietnamese dish. Serving this dish with raw betel leaves ties it all back into its *bo la lot* inspiration. We use prawn crackers instead of toast to make this dish a bit more Asian.

VIETNAMESE STEAK TARTARE

Serves 4

DRESSING
85 ml (2¾ fl oz) fish sauce
1 tablespoon caster (superfine) sugar
1 tablespoon lime juice
1¼ tablespoons white vinegar
1½ teaspoons chilli oil
55 ml (1¾ fl oz) grapeseed oil
½ tablespoon of ót tuóng (Essentials, page 244)

Whisk all of the ingredients together in a bowl and set aside.

THE REST
400 g (14 oz) piece of good-quality tartare-grade beef
30 leaves coriander (cilantro), thinly sliced
30 leaves Vietnamese mint, thinly sliced
30 leaves round leaf mint, thinly sliced
4 leaves sawtooth coriander (cilantro), thinly sliced
20 Thai basil leaves, thinly sliced
2 lemongrass stems, pale part only, very thinly sliced
1 bunch chives, finely chopped
4 tablespoons fried shallots (Essentials, page 242)
4 free-range egg yolks
prawn crackers, to serve

Remove all visible sinew from the beef and then, with a sharp knife, chop coarsely into very small pieces about 4 mm (¼ inch) wide. You don't want to go too fine, as a good tartare has a bit of texture and 'chew'. Put the beef in a bowl and add the herbs, lemongrass and chives. Add about 125 ml (4 fl oz/½ cup) of the dressing. Mix everything until well combined.

TO SERVE

Divide the mixture among four plates and heap into mounds. Top with fried shallots. Make a small dent in the middle of each mound and fill with one egg yolk. Serve with the prawn crackers.

This dish is based on a Thai green papaya salad. Green papaya salads are up there with the most iconic salads of the world such as the Caesar, insalata caprese and salad Niçoise. I wanted to create a Thai-influenced dish, and this one draws on my days at Longrain, one of Sydney's most iconic Thai restaurants. Thai food really blends well with ceviche dishes. Together, they provide balance and strength. This salad is like ceviche on steroids. The texture of the raw fish, the cooling papaya and the crunch of the tostada works really well. The creaminess of the guacamole completes this dish and rounds out the palate.

KINGFISH SASHIMI TOSTADA with GREEN PAPAYA and GUACAMOLE

Makes 2

GREEN NAHM JIM
2 coriander (cilantro) stems, washed, finely chopped
3 small long green chillies, roughly chopped
5 Thai green chillies, seeded
½ lemongrass stem, pale part only, finely chopped
10 g (¼ oz) galangal, finely chopped
3 small garlic cloves, peeled
80 g (2¾ oz) palm sugar
125 ml (4 fl oz/½ cup) lime juice
100 ml (3½ fl oz) fish sauce

In a large mortar and pestle, pound the coriander stems, chillies, lemongrass, galangal and garlic with a little sea salt until a paste forms. Add the palm sugar and continue to pound everything until the sugar dissolves. Add the lime juice and fish sauce. Stir well to combine and adjust seasoning to taste.

TOSTADAS
vegetable oil, for deep-frying
2 x 20 cm (8 inch) white corn tortillas

To make the tostadas (fried tortillas), fill a deep-fryer or large saucepan one-third full with vegetable oil and heat to 180°C (350°F) or until a cube of bread dropped into the oil turns golden in 15 seconds. Cut the tortillas into quarters and fry until crispy and golden. Remove with a slotted spoon, drain on paper towels and leave to cool. Transfer the tostadas to an airtight container lined with paper towel until ready to use.

GUACAMOLE
2 ripe avocados
zest of ½ lime
juice of 2 limes
120 g (4¼ oz) sour cream
4 tablespoons olive oil
½ teaspoon xanthan gum
1 teaspoon ground cumin
3 garlic cloves
1 bunch coriander (cilantro), roughly chopped
1 teaspoon salt
2 tablespoons fish sauce

Place all the ingredients in the bowl of a food processor, add 3½ tablespoons water and blend on a high speed to form a smooth paste. To prevent the guacamole from oxidising and turning brown, store in a bowl covered with plastic wrap that is in direct contact with the guacamole.

CEVICHE

100 g (3½ oz) sashimi-grade kingfish
200 g (7 oz) piece of green papaya, peeled, seeded
and cut into thin matchsticks
1 red Asian shallot, thinly sliced
15 coriander (cilantro) leaves
15 Vietnamese mint leaves
10 Thai basil leaves, torn just prior to assembling
the salad
30 g (1 oz) ocean trout roe
baby shiso leaves, to garnish

Combine the kingfish, papaya, shallot, coriander,
Vietnamese mint and Thai basil leaves in a salad
bowl. Spoon about 100 ml (3½ fl oz) of the green
nahm jim into the salad bowl and mix gently with
clean hands until well combined.

TO SERVE

When you're ready to plate up, spoon the
guacamole into a piping (icing) bag. Divide the
tortilla quarters between two plates and evenly
distribute the salad on top. Make sure each quarter
gets some kingfish, along with a bit of salad. Garnish
with dots of guacamole and trout roe and finish with
a few baby shiso leaves. Serve the remaining salad
on the side and allow people to help themselves.

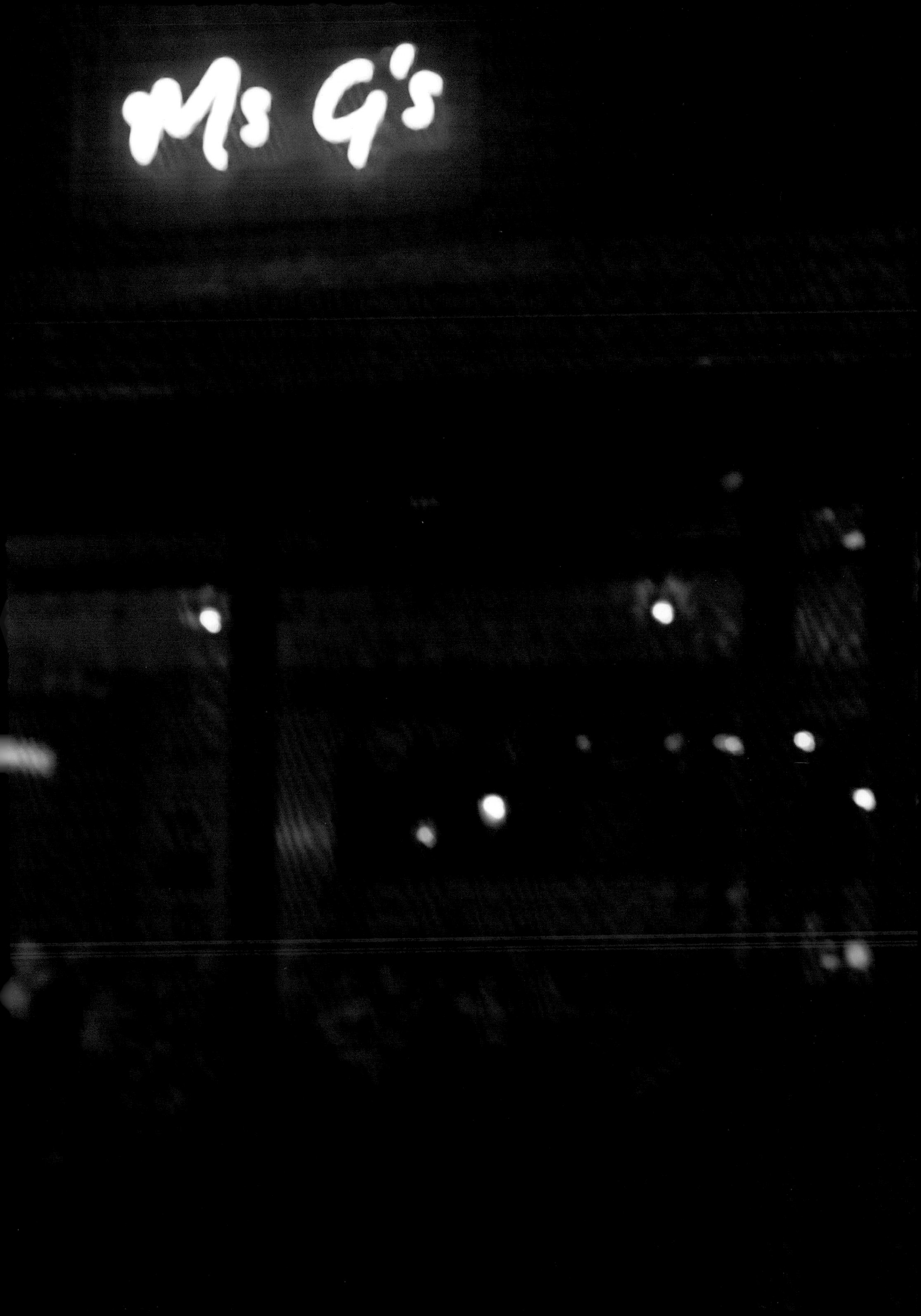
Ms G's

Did I mention that I like offal? I want to change people's minds about it... it can be awesome. I always sneak an offal recipe onto every restaurant menu I work on. This is a dish that satisfies ourselves as chefs – because we like eating things that are more obscure, but I also think it appeals to people who really know food. This dish is, essentially, boiled offal, mixed with loads of chilli oil, soy and vinegar and covered in green shallots, sesame seeds and coriander. The name of the salad refers to a well-balanced relationship. For one to work, there needs to be a balance of light and passive (yin) and heavier or stronger (yang) elements.

SALAD of HUSBAND and WIFE

Serves about 6

TRIPE AND PIG'S EARS
4 litres (140 fl oz/16 cups) Chinese masterstock (Essentials, page 234)
200 g (7 oz) honeycomb tripe
6 pig's ears

Bring the stock to the boil in a large saucepan and gently lower in the tripe and pig's ears. Bring the stock back to the boil and simmer for 3 hours, or until the tripe is tender to the touch and the ears are slightly tender, but not falling apart.

Remove the tripe and pig's ears from the masterstock and transfer to a tray. Leave to cool, then refrigerate. When firm and cold, thinly slice both the tripe and ears into thin strips, cover and refrigerate until ready to serve.

DRESSING
100 ml (3½ fl oz) white soy sauce
2 tablespoons mirin
2 tablespoons white vinegar
2 tablespoons sesame oil
2 tablespoons chilli oil
2 teaspoons ground Sichuan pepper

Combine all the ingredients with 3 tablespoons of water in a bowl. Set aside.

SALAD
1 telegraph (long) cucumber, seeded, cut into thin matchsticks
100 g (3½ oz) compressed celery (Essentials, page 245), cut into 4 cm x 2 mm (1½ x ¹⁄₁₆ inch) batons
3 small long red chillies, cut into very thin long strips
1 bunch coriander (cilantro), roughly chopped, including stems
3 spring onions (scallions), thinly sliced
roasted pumpkin seeds (pepitas), to garnish

In a bowl combine the tripe, pig's ears and salad ingredients (except the pepitas) and mix well. Give the dressing a quick whisk and add to the salad. Toss well, top with the pepitas and serve.

Buddha's Delight is a broad term. In some parts of Asia it's a stir-fry, in others, it's a raw salad. I wanted to make a really cool vegetarian salad and the whole basis of anything I do that's vegetarian is that it must be complete by itself. A good vegetarian dish should be able to stand up to any meat dish.

BUDDHA'S DELIGHT

Serves 4

DRESSING
145 ml (4¾ fl oz) soy sauce
4 tablespoons sugar syrup (Essentials, page 240)
1½ tablespoons Chinkiang black vinegar
2 tablespoons grapeseed oil
1¼ tablespoons sesame oil

Whisk all the ingredients in a bowl with 125 ml (4 fl oz/½ cup) water until well combined. Keeps in the fridge for up to 2 weeks.

BLACK VINEGAR SOY NOODLES
2½ tablespoons light soy sauce
1¾ tablespoons Chinkiang black vinegar
2 teaspoons caster (superfine) sugar
½ garlic clove, finely grated
½ teaspoon finely grated ginger
3 g (⅛ oz) agar-agar

Mix all the ingredients together with 100 ml (3½ fl oz) water in a saucepan over a high heat. Bring to the boil and simmer for 3 minutes. Immediately pour the liquid into a small slab tin.

Carefully transfer the tin to the fridge and leave until the liquid sets to a firm jelly. Unmould it from the tin and cut into noodles about 6 cm (2½ inches) long and 3 mm (⅛ inch) thick. Keep them in the fridge until you're ready to assemble the dish.

THE REST
50 g (1¾ oz) pickled carrot (see Pickling liquid recipe, Essentials, page 241)
50 g (1¾ oz) pickled daikon (see Pickling liquid recipe, Essentials, page 241)
50 g (1¾ oz) fresh black fungi, thinly sliced into strips
½ telegraph (long) cucumber, seeded, cut into thin matchsticks
2 small long red chillies, cut into thin matchsticks
100 g (3½ oz) firm Chinese five-spice tofu, cut into 3 cm x 3 mm (1¼ x ⅛ inch) batons
100 g (3½ oz) bean sprouts, blanched, refreshed in iced water and drained
30 g (1 oz) dried wakame, reconstituted in water and drained
40 coriander (cilantro) leaves
4 spring onions (scallions), finely shredded
100 g (3½ oz) salted, roasted cashew nuts, chopped

Combine all the ingredients, except the cashews, in a bowl and add the noodles. Spoon as much dressing as you think you'll need onto the salad and mix everything with clean hands. Taste it and check if you need to add a bit more dressing – everything should be coated well. Divide among 4 plates, top with the cashews and serve.

HONG HACK
If you can't find Chinese five-spice tofu at your Asian supermarket, buy plain firm tofu and rub it with a mixture of oil, salt and Chinese five-spice and leave it to infuse.

This dish was inspired by my mum and was on the menu at her restaurant Than Binh. Mum has this A4 page of 'specials' that have been pretty much the same for about eight years. One of the dishes combines crispy pork belly with pineapple and this is my take on it. This is not a traditional Vietnamese dish, but something she came up with. In my version, I add calamari for the surf 'n' turf factor, and for texture.

SALAD of CRISPY PORK BELLY, CALAMARI and PINEAPPLE with GINGER NUOC CHAM

Serves 2 as an entrée

BRAISED PORK BELLY
1.5 kg (3 lb 5 oz) pork belly, rib bones removed, skin on
6 litres (210 fl oz/24 cups) Chinese masterstock (Essentials, page 234)

Follow the method for the mini pork banh mi recipe (recipe, page 54) up until you are ready to slice. Cut 200 g (7 oz) of the pork belly into 1.5 cm (⅝ inch) cubes.

DRESSING
200 ml (7 fl oz) nuoc cham (Essentials, page 244)
1 teaspoon finely grated ginger
½ teaspoon finely grated garlic
1½ tablespoons fish sauce
2 teaspoons lime juice

Whisk all the ingredients together in a bowl until well combined.

THE REST
vegetable oil, for frying
200 g (7 oz) piece of cleaned calamari, cut into thin strips
½ pineapple, skin and core removed, cut into 4 cm x 3 mm (1½ x ⅛ inch) strips
1 baby cos (romaine) lettuce, outer leaves removed, finely shredded
10 betel leaves, finely shredded
20 round leaf mint leaves
20 Vietnamese mint leaves
crushed corn nuts, to garnish

Add a little oil to a frying pan and heat over a high heat. When the pan is hot, shallow-fry the calamari for 1–2 minutes until just cooked. Season with salt, remove from the pan, cover and keep warm.

Fill a deep-fryer or large heavy-based saucepan one-third full with oil and heat to 200°C (400°F) or until a cube of bread dropped into the oil turns golden in 5 seconds. When the oil is hot, deep-fry the pork belly cubes for about 3 minutes until crisp and golden. Remove with a slotted spoon and drain on paper towels. Keep warm.

In a bowl combine the calamari and pork with all the remaining ingredients except the corn nuts. Dress with 150–200 ml (5–7 fl oz) of the dressing and toss to combine. Divide among two plates and garnish with crushed corn nuts.

HONG HACK
Corn nuts are corn kernels that have been hydrated and deep-fried. You can buy them at specialist Asian or Latin grocery stores. They're not absolutely essential in this dish, but they add a nice crunch.

I love ranch dressing. I wanted to include it on the menu at Ms G's. Adding miso adds a more umami depth of flavour and gave me an excuse to put it on the menu. This recipe goes well with any seafood, especially raw seafood, so feel free to play around with different kinds of sashimi. The preserved lemon adds fragrance and the compressed celery adds crunch and is a classic pairing with ranch dressing. Kombu adds an extra dimension of texture.

SEARED CUTTLEFISH with PRESERVED LEMON, CELERY, MISO RANCH and KOMBU

Serves 2

MISO RANCH DRESSING
100 g (3½ oz) sour cream
100 g (3½ oz) Japanese mayonnaise
2½ tablespoons milk
2½ tablespoons yuzu juice
60 g (2¼ oz) white miso paste
½ teaspoon yuzukoshō
1 tablespoon onion powder
½ tablespoon garlic powder

Whisk all the ingredients together in a bowl with a pinch of salt until well combined. Refrigerate until ready to serve.

THE REST
200 g (7 oz) cleaned cuttlefish tubes
1 tablespoon vegetable oil
50 g (1¾ oz) compressed celery (Essentials, page 245)
1 preserved lemon, rind only
10 g (¼ oz) shio kombu
1 small handful of baby coriander (cilantro) leaves
2 tablespoons trout roe

Lie the cuttlefish tubes flat, underside upward, and score them with lines 5 mm (¼ inch) apart. Slice into 3 cm (1¼ inch) pieces. The end result: bite-sized pieces, each scored with parallel lines. Season with a little salt.

Add the oil to a large frying pan and heat over a high heat. When the oil is searingly hot, add the cuttlefish, scored side down. Fry for 25 seconds then carefully flip each piece over and cook for

20 seconds. The cuttlefish should be nicely caramelised on the scored side. Remove from the pan and keep warm.

TO SERVE

Slice the compressed celery against the grain into 2 mm (¹⁄₁₆ inch) pieces. Slice the preserved lemon skin into thin matchsticks. Slick a thick layer of miso ranch dressing on two separate plates. Top with the cooked cuttlefish pieces, then add some celery and strips of preserved lemon and shio kombu. Top with baby coriander leaves, then spoon some trout roe on top, and all over the plate as well.

HONG HACKS
Ask your fishmonger to clean the cuttlefish tubes.

Yuzukoshō is a fermented paste made from chilli peppers, yuzu peel and salt, and is available from Japanese grocery stores. Yuzukoshō is kind of irreplaceable, which means you're screwed, so just omit it.

PRAWN TOAST with YUZU MAYONNAISE, CORIANDER and MINT

Serves 6 as a snack

PRAWN MOUSSE

600 g (1 lb 5 oz) prawn (shrimp) meat
1 egg white
1 tablespoon sesame oil
3 teaspoons sugar
2 teaspoons fine salt
2 tablespoons thinly sliced coriander (cilantro) stems

To make the mousse, put all the ingredients in the bowl of a food processor and pulse to create a coarse-looking paste. Resist the urge to make it too smooth, because you still want chunks of prawn for texture. Refrigerate the mixture for at least 2 hours to firm up.

THE REST

1 large loaf of sourdough
sesame seeds, for sprinkling
vegetable oil, for deep-frying
yuzu mayonnaise (Essentials, page 240)

Cut the ends off the bread and slice it into 8 mm (⅜ inch) slices. Using a butter knife, spread the prawn mousse evenly over the slices until you reach an even 1 cm (½ inch) layer. Sprinkle the tops with sesame seeds.

Fill a heavy-based saucepan one-third full with oil and heat to 180°C (350°F) or until a cube of bread dropped into the oil turns golden in 15 seconds. Fry each piece of toast one at a time for about 5 minutes or until the toast is golden and the prawn mousse is fully cooked. Drain on paper towels then cut each toast into 4–5 slices. Take this opportunity to check if the mousse is fully cooked. If it could do with a little bit longer, throw the toast back into the deep-fryer and give it another minute or two.

THE SALAD

1 small handful of coriander (cilantro) leaves, picked
1 small handful of round leaf mint leaves
1 small handful of Vietnamese mint leaves
2 spring onions (scallions), thinly sliced
2½ tablespoons nuoc cham (Essentials, page 244)

Mix the salad herbs and spring onions in a bowl, then dress with the nuoc cham.

TO SERVE

Top each piece of toast with some yuzu mayonnaise and garnish with fresh herb salad.

This dish is another happy marriage. Australians love sang choi bao – it's a classic suburban Chinese restaurant dish that everyone grew up eating. And what better to pair it with than lamb, Australia's favourite protein. Eggplant works really well with lamb, so this dish is just a combination of best mates. Prepare to marinate the lamb a day ahead.

SANG CHOI BAO of SICHUAN LAMB with SMOKED EGGPLANT NAHM PRIK

Serves about 12

EGGPLANT NAHM PRIK
1 kg (2 lb 4 oz) large eggplants (aubergines)
1 pickled jalapeño pepper, roughly chopped
10 coriander (cilantro) roots, washed
2 garlic cloves, peeled
15 g (½ oz) small long red chillies, roughly chopped
50 g (1¾ oz) white miso paste
5 g (⅛ oz) bonito flakes (katsuoboshi)
juice of 1 lime
2 tablespoons fish sauce

Roast the eggplants over an open flame (a gas hob works well) until the skin is nicely charred all over and the flesh is soft.

Transfer them (blistered skin and all) to a bowl and cover with plastic wrap to steam them for 20 minutes. When they are cool enough to handle, carefully remove and discard the charred skin.

Put the flesh into the bowl of a food processor and whizz along with the rest of the ingredients. Taste it. It should be sour, salty and smoky. Adjust the seasoning to your taste with more lime or fish sauce if necessary.

MARINATED LAMB
4 garlic cloves, peeled
250 g (9 oz) fermented tofu (fuyu)
3½ tablespoons Knorr Liquid Seasoning
150 ml (5 fl oz) shaoxing wine
2½ teaspoons bicarbonate of soda (baking soda)
1 kg (2 lb 4 oz) boneless lamb leg, all sinew removed, diced into 1 cm (½ inch) pieces

Blend all the ingredients except the lamb in a food processor until a smooth paste forms. Transfer to a bowl, add the lamb and toss well to coat. Marinate overnight in the fridge, covered, or for at least 2 hours.

THE REST
vegetable oil, for frying
kernels from 4 cobs of corn
1 bunch garlic chives, snipped into 5 mm (¼ inch) lengths
150 g (5½ oz) unsalted roasted peanuts
100 ml (3½ fl oz) maple syrup
100 g (3½ oz) Lao Gan Ma chilli oil (with peanuts)
baby cos (romaine) lettuce leaves, to serve
sprigs of coriander (cilantro), mint, Vietnamese mint and baby shiso leaves, to garnish

Add a little oil to a hot wok over a high heat. Start by frying the lamb in batches. Be sure not to overcrowd the wok, otherwise you'll end up with stewed meat rather than nicely caramelised pieces.

Fry each batch for 3–4 minutes, until three-quarters cooked. Once you've stir-fried all the lamb, return it to the wok and add the corn, garlic chives and peanuts and stir-fry for 1 minute. Add the maple syrup and reduce the liquid in the wok by half. Finally, add the chilli sauce and cook for a further 1 minute.

Serve the lamb in a bowl, with the lettuce cups, herbs and eggplant on the side. Help yourselves!

EGG NOODLES with BRAISED DUCK, XO SAUCE and SLOW-COOKED EGG

Serves 4

BRAISED DUCK
1 whole fresh duck (1.8 kg/4 lb)
6 litres (210 fl oz/24 cups) Chinese masterstock (Essentials, page 234)
3 tablespoons oyster sauce

Preheat the oven to 160°C (315°F/Gas 2–3). Wash the duck. Cut the wing tips off and discard, then place the duck in a large ovenproof braising saucepan. Pour in enough masterstock to cover the duck and bring to the boil. Once it has reached a rolling boil, remove from the heat. Put a lid on the saucepan and transfer it to the oven for 3 hours.

After 3 hours, the meat should come off the bone easily. Carefully lift out the duck from the braising liquid and set aside to cool. When cool enough to handle (but still warm), remove the skin and pick the meat off the bones.

Mix the oyster sauce with 2 tablespoons of masterstock and use to brush the duck meat. Set aside and keep warm.

NOODLE SAUCE
300 ml (10½ fl oz) oyster sauce
2 tablespoons melted duck or goose fat
1½ tablespoons Chinkiang black vinegar

In a bowl, whisk all the ingredients until well combined.

THE REST
480 g (1 lb 1 oz) thin egg noodles
4 tablespoons XO sauce (Essentials, page 239)
4 slow-cooked eggs (Essentials, page 241)
1 telegraph (long) cucumber, seeded, cut into thin matchsticks, to garnish
2 spring onions (scallions), thinly sliced, to garnish
40 coriander (cilantro) leaves, to garnish

Blanch the egg noodles in a large saucepan of boiling water for 30 seconds. Drain, then transfer to a large mixing bowl. Give the noodle sauce a quick whisk, then add 200 ml (7 fl oz) of it to the bowl of noodles. Using tongs or chopsticks, mix the noodles into the sauce and divide between four bowls.

Top each bowl with a tablespoon of XO sauce and some braised duck. Crack open an egg on top of each bowl and garnish with cucumber, spring onions and coriander.

HONG HACKS
If you don't have a saucepan large enough to fit the duck or the pan is too big to fit in the oven, use a roasting tin instead. Place the duck on a roasting rack and fill the tin almost to the top with masterstock. Completely seal the tray with foil before baking.

Forgot to make the XO sauce? Buy it. This spicy umami-packed sauce is available from Asian grocery stores.

Not enough time to slow-cook the eggs? Just top with a fried egg. You can also lose the egg... just don't tell me about it.

Bali has a special place in my heart because my wife is Indonesian and we were married in Bali. Whenever we are there we go to Jimbaran Bay. It's quite touristy, but we don't care because it doesn't get much better than eating freshly caught, grilled seafood on the beach with sand between your toes. Sambal matah is a traditional Balinese sambal that (unlike many other kinds of sambal) is uncooked. In that respect, it's much like a salsa, but a lot more intense. It is perfect with grilled fish or shellfish such as lobster and prawns. The sambal is quite spicy, so the watermelon and cucumber salad adds cooling freshness to the dish. Good fish to use for this recipe are baby snapper, flounder or baby barramundi. Ask your fishmonger to scale and gut it.

GRILLED WHOLE FISH with SAMBAL MATAH, WATERMELON and CUCUMBER

Serves 4–6 as part of a meal, depending on the size of the fish

SAMBAL MATAH
10 red Asian shallots, thinly sliced
5 bird's eye chillies, thinly sliced
5 kaffir lime leaves, very thinly sliced
2 lemongrass stems, pale part only, very thinly sliced
2 garlic cloves, very finely chopped
5 small long red chillies, finely chopped
1 teaspoon shrimp paste
juice of 2 limes
1 teaspoon salt
2½ tablespoons fish sauce
2 teaspoons caster (superfine) sugar
1½ tablespoons coconut oil
100 ml (3½ fl oz) grapeseed oil

Mix all the ingredients together in a bowl until well combined. Set aside.

SALAD
100 g (3½ oz) seedless watermelon, cut into 1 cm (½ inch) cubes
1 Lebanese cucumber, seeded, cut into 1 cm (½ inch) cubes
5 coriander (cilantro) leaves, thinly sliced
5 mint leaves, thinly sliced
5 Vietnamese mint leaves, thinly sliced
2 tablespoons nuoc cham (Essentials, page 244)

Toss the watermelon, cucumber and herb leaves together in a bowl and dress with nuoc cham.

1 whole fish (see intro above), weighing about 750 g (1 lb 10 oz)
vegetable oil, for brushing
lime wedges, to serve

Season the fish with salt and brush it with vegetable oil. Heat a chargrill pan or barbecue to very hot, which will help prevent the skin from sticking. Put the fish on the grill and, after about 4 minutes, carefully flip it over with a large spatula. It should be nicely charred. Cook the other side for another 4 minutes or until the fish is cooked through.

Transfer to a serving dish and spoon some sambal matah and the watermelon salad over the top of the fish. Serve with wedges of lime.

This is a really cool dish because it embodies what the food at Ms G's is all about: it's a combination of different Asian cuisines combined to create something else. This recipe is our kind-of 'Peking duck' dish: the components are all there... crisp, tasty meat, the freshness of a salad element, a potent sauce... all wrapped up in those super-addictive pancakes. It's Chinese, Korean and Vietnamese all in the one bite. The gel was created because nuoc cham (while flavour-wise works perfectly with this dish) was too liquid and would run down to your elbows as you ate it. Using agar-agar to create a gel fixed that. This recipe is in large-ish proportions because it's perfect party food. Also, most people can't just stop at one or two. Simply divide down the quantities and adjust the cooking times to make this dish suitable for smaller numbers. Prepare a day in advance to allow the pork belly to dry out before roasting.

CRISPY PORK BELLY PANCAKES with CUCUMBER KIMCHI and NUOC CHAM

Serves about 12

ROASTED PORK BELLY

1 piece of pork belly, around 5 kg (11 lb 4 oz)
30 g (1 oz) bicarbonate of soda (baking soda)
150 g (5½ oz) salt
2½ tablespoons caster (superfine) sugar
35 g (1¼ oz) Chinese five-spice

Fill a large wok or saucepan with water and bring to the boil. Blanch the pork belly for 3 minutes, then drain and transfer to a tray, skin side up. Pierce all over the skin with a skewer. Next, mix the bicarbonate of soda with roughly two-thirds of the salt and rub this over the skin. Combine the sugar, Chinese five-spice and remaining salt. Turn the pork belly over and rub the spice mix into the underside. Set aside to rest, uncovered, in a cool, dry place for 24 hours. If you can't do this, store it overnight in the fridge on a rack with a drip tray, uncovered.

CUCUMBER KIMCHI

1 kg (2 lb 4 oz) salted cucumber (Essentials, page 241)
½ bunch spring onions (scallions), thinly sliced
½ onion, thinly sliced
4 tablespoons Korean chilli powder
2 tablespoons fish sauce
2½ tablespoons sugar
3 tablespoons sesame oil
2 tablespoons rice wine vinegar
½ tablespoon chilli oil
1 tablespoon finely grated garlic
1 small long red chilli, very finely chopped
2 tablespoons sesame seeds

Wearing food prep gloves or similar (trust me, you don't want this on your hands), mix all the ingredients together in a bowl, making sure you massage the cucumbers really well. Cover and set aside in the fridge.

When you're ready to cook the pork, preheat the oven to 240°C (475°F/Gas 8). Put the pork belly on a rack in a roasting tin and roast for 30 minutes. Turn the heat down to 180°C (350°F/Gas 4) and continue roasting for 45 minutes. Remove from the oven and, using a knife, scrape off any burnt bits and any excess salt. Keep warm.

TO SERVE
Peking duck pancake wrappers
sprigs of coriander (cilantro), Vietnamese mint,
Thai basil and round leaf mint
nuoc cham gel (Essentials, page 244)

Place a large bamboo steamer over a saucepan of simmering water and steam the pancake wrappers until soft. Wrap in a tea towel (dish towel) to keep them warm as they have a tendency to dry out and go hard.

Carve the roasted pork belly into thick slices and arrange on a serving plate. Serve with the warm pancakes, herbs, nuoc cham gel and cucumber kimchi. This is a fun DIY dish as people can have a little more or less of the stuff they love.

HONG HACK
Substitute the roasted pork for any preferred meat, or if you're really stuck for time with a party of people about to drop in on you, sub in a side of roast pork from your local Chinese BBQ restaurant. I won't tell.

This dish is inspired by my time eating in the hawker centres of Singapore. One of the dishes I always get is sambal stingray. I love the gelatinous quality of stingray mixed with the sweet/spicy flavour of the sambal belacan. This sambal is a cooked-down chilli paste, heady with pungent shrimp paste (belacan). The shrimp paste really gives it a punch that stands up well to the earthiness of barramundi. Other firm-fleshed fish such as (sustainably sourced) Patagonian toothfish, mulloway or flounder also works well. Prawns and squid work well too.

ROASTED SAMBAL BARRAMUNDI

Serves 3

SAMBAL BELACAN

500 g (1 lb 2 oz) small long red chillies, deseeded
30 g (1 oz) candlenuts
2 large onions, coarsely chopped
10 garlic cloves, peeled
2 cm (¾ inch) piece fresh turmeric
2 teaspoons chilli flakes
250 g (9 oz) sambal chilli with prawn (shrimp)
100 g (3½ oz) shrimp paste in soya bean oil
1 tablespoon shrimp paste
3 tablespoons caster (superfine) sugar
1 tablespoon salt
100 ml (3½ fl oz) fish sauce
500 ml (17 fl oz/2 cups) vegetable oil
2½ tablespoons chilli oil

You may need to do this in batches, depending on how powerful your food processor is. Put all the ingredients into the bowl of a food processor, except for half (250 ml/9 fl oz) the vegetable oil and chilli oil. Blend until a smooth paste forms.

Heat a large heavy-based saucepan over a high heat and add the remaining vegetable oil. When hot, add the paste and fry it for 2 minutes. Reduce the heat to medium and add the chilli oil. Reduce the heat to low and simmer, stirring often, for about 2 hours or until the paste is dark red and the oil has started to split and rise to the surface. Taste the sambal. It should not taste of raw onions and garlic but instead be hot, a little sweet and a little salty.

THE BARRAMUNDI

3 x 200 g (7 oz) barramundi fillets (pin-boned, skin off)
vegetable oil, for frying
lime wedges, to serve
coriander (cilantro) sprigs, for garnish

Marinate the barramundi with a tablespoon of sambal per fillet and refrigerate for 2 hours for the flavours to soak in.

Preheat the oven to 160°C (315°F/Gas 2–3). Season the barramundi on both sides with salt and pepper. Heat a large heavy-based, ovenproof skillet over a high heat, add a little vegetable oil and sear the fillets for about 2 minutes on each side.

TO SERVE

Spoon a tablespoon of sambal on top of the fillet, making sure it's evenly spread. Transfer the whole pan to the oven and bake for about 5 minutes, depending on the thickness of the fish. To test if the fish is done, insert a metal skewer into the thickest part of the fillet; when done the skewer will feel very hot to touch.

Transfer the cooked fish to a plate and garnish with lime halves and coriander sprigs. Serve with hot rice and cold beer.

Who doesn't love fried chicken? Even vegetarians like fried chicken. Baby chickens are quick to cook, which keeps everything tender. This is a simple dish, but really pleasing. I really like Korean fried chicken and will visit any place in Chinatown if there's the slightest possibility it could be good. Korean Fried Chicken (KFC) influenced this recipe.

FRIED BABY CHICKEN with KIMCHI MAYONNAISE

Serves 4

MARINADE
300 ml (10½ fl oz) Shaoxing wine
3 tablespoons salt
1 tablespoon sugar
2 garlic cloves, finely grated
1 teaspoon finely grated ginger

Whisk all the marinade ingredients together in a bowl until the sugar and salt dissolve. Put the chicken pieces in a bowl, add the marinade and toss to coat. Cover with plastic wrap and leave to marinate for at least 4 hours. Overnight in the fridge is even better.

COATING MIXTURE
100 g (3½ oz/⅔ cup) wheat starch
100 g (3½ oz/⅔ cup) plain (all-purpose) flour
100 g (3½ oz) cornflour (cornstarch)
100 g (3½ oz) rice flour
3 tablespoons onion powder
3 tablespoons garlic powder

Mix everything together in a bowl until combined.

KIMCHI MAYO
100 g (3½ oz) kimchi (store-bought)
300 g (10½ oz) Japanese mayonnaise

To make the kimchi mayo, purée the kimchi in a food processor until smooth. Transfer to a bowl, add the mayonnaise and whisk to combine. Set aside.

THE SPATCHCOCKS
2 whole spatchcocks (poussin), cut up into wings, breasts, thighs and drumsticks
vegetable oil, for deep-frying
2 tablespoons spicy salt (Essentials, page 243)

Fill a deep-fryer or large heavy-based saucepan one-third full with oil and heat to 170°C (325°F) or until a cube of bread dropped into the oil turns golden in 20 seconds. Remove the chicken pieces from the marinade and cover each piece in the coating mixture until it feels dry. Deep-fry in batches in the hot oil for 5–6 minutes, or until the skin is golden and crispy. Remove with a slotted spoon, drain on paper towels and sprinkle with spicy salt. Serve immediately with the kimchi mayo.

Lamb ribs are seriously underrated as a cut. We always think to go with pork, but lamb ribs are fatty, sticky and gelatinous – everything you want in a rib and also, the perfect beer companion. The sweet and sour sauce keeps well in the fridge and is handy to have on hand for when the mood strikes.

SWEET and SOUR LAMB RIBS

Serves 4–6

SWEET AND SOUR SAUCE
500 g (1 lb 2 oz) caster (superfine) sugar
150 ml (5 fl oz) Chinkiang black vinegar
170 ml (5½ fl oz/⅔ cup) fish sauce
150 g (5 oz) soy paste
3 lemongrass stems, pale part only,
very finely chopped
2 tablespoons finely chopped ginger
10 garlic cloves, finely chopped
2 small long red chillies, very finely chopped
2 tablespoons ground cumin

To make the caramel, add the sugar and 100 ml (3½ fl oz) water to a heavy-based saucepan over a high heat. Resist the urge to stir, just allow the heat to begin to transform the sugar. Gently swirl the water to move things around a little bit, and use a wet pastry brush to brush down the sides if crystals start to appear.

Once a light caramel is achieved (about 245°C/475°F on a sugar thermometer), add the remaining ingredients. Be careful as the mixture may spit. At this point, the sugar will start to solidify. Bring the mixture to the boil again and simmer until the sugar has re-melted and you have a uniform sauce. Cool, then transfer to an airtight container and set aside.

LAMB RIBS
5 racks of lamb ribs
6 litres (210 fl oz/24 cups) Chinese masterstock
(Essentials, page 234)
vegetable oil, for deep-frying
1 small handful of coriander (cilantro) leaves,
roughly chopped, to garnish
1 small handful of mint leaves, roughly chopped,
to garnish
1 small handful of Vietnamese mint leaves,
roughly chopped
lime wedges, to serve

Preheat the oven to 160°C (315°F/Gas 2–3). Put the lamb ribs in a large ovenproof braising saucepan, cover with the masterstock and heat over a high heat. When the stock reaches boiling point, remove from the heat, cover with a lid, and transfer the dish to the oven. Bake for 3½ hours.

You can tell when the meat is done as it will be meltingly tender and falling away from the bone. Leave the ribs in the liquid until they are cool enough to handle. Spread them out on a tray, cover with plastic wrap and refrigerate overnight.

The next day, cut the ribs into individual pieces. Heat the oil in a deep-fryer to 180°C (350°F). Deep-fry the ribs in batches for about 4 minutes, or until they go dark and crispy. Put the ribs in a bowl with the herbs and a generous amount of the sweet and sour sauce. Toss to coat, making sure you coat the ribs generously with the sauce.

TO SERVE

Transfer to a platter, scatter with the herbs and serve with lime wedges.

I don't know how this dish got the following it has now. It's totally unbalanced, super sweet and salty and fully over the top. Nevertheless, it remains the top-selling dessert at Ms G's by far.

   This dessert came about because I wanted to create something nobody else had. I was a heavy pot smoker back in high school and I thought about the ridiculous things I'd combine to eat because they seemed like the best idea ever (at the time). This dish originally consisted of doughnut ice cream, peanut butter, Mars Bar slice, passionfruit marshmallow, pretzel praline and raspberry sauce. After months of being obsessed with watching EpicMealTime on YouTube, I added candied bacon, replaced the marshmallow with deep-fried banana fritter, mixed the peanut butter with dulce de leche and switched the pretzels for potato chips. I don't know what happens when people eat this dish (probably the beginnings of a diabetic coma), but they tend to go a bit crazy.

STONER'S
DELIGHT

STONER'S DELIGHT

Serves 6–8 (or 4, depending on how stoned you are)

DOUGHNUT ICE CREAM

7 egg yolks
175 g (6 oz) caster (superfine) sugar
675 ml (23¼ fl oz) milk
190 ml (6½ fl oz) thin (pouring) cream
1 teaspoon ground cinnamon
6 cinnamon doughnuts, cut into small pieces

Put the egg yolks and sugar in a bowl and whisk for about 5 minutes, or until airy and thick. Add the milk, cream and cinnamon to a saucepan over a high heat and bring to the boil. Whisking continuously, slowly add the hot custard to the yolk–sugar mixture. Continue whisking until everything is well combined.

Add the doughnut pieces and, using a hand-held blender, mash them into the mixture. Remove from the heat and leave to cool. Churn in an ice-cream machine according to the manufacturer's instructions. Spoon into a container and store in the freezer, covered.

POTATO CHIP PRALINE

200 g (7 oz) caster (superfine) sugar
200 g (7 oz) liquid glucose
250 g (9 oz) your favourite salted potato chips

Line a baking tray with baking paper. To make the caramel, add the sugar and 2½ tablespoons water to a heavy-based saucepan over a high heat. Resist the urge to stir, just allow the heat to begin to transform the sugar. Gently swirl the water to move things around a little bit, and use a wet pastry brush to brush down the side if crystals start to appear.

Once the mixture reaches a light blonde colour (about 150°C/300°F on a sugar thermometer), add the potato chips and stir quickly to combine. You need to cover the chips with the caramel. Quickly spread the praline over the prepared tray then leave it to cool and harden. When the praline is solid, break it up with a pestle to create random-sized shards. Transfer to an airtight container and store in the freezer.

CANDIED BACON

6 belly bacon slices, about 3 mm thick x 10 cm long (⅛ x 4 inch)
brown sugar, for dusting

Preheat the oven to 155°C (310°F/Gas 2). Line a baking tray with baking paper and then spread the bacon In a single layer (with no overlapping) on the tray. Sprinkle the bacon liberally with brown sugar (at least 1 tablespoon per slice… remember this dessert is for stoners).

Cover the whole surface of the bacon with the sugar, then bake for 15–20 minutes, or until the bacon is caramelised and crisp. When cooled, store in an airtight container in the freezer.

MARS BAR SLICE

4 x 55 g (2 oz) Mars Bars, cut into 1 cm (½ inch) pieces
120 g (4¼ oz) unsalted butter, plus 15 g (½ oz) for the topping
120 g (4¼ oz/4 cups) Rice Bubbles
110 g (3¾ oz) dark chocolate, broken up into coarse chunks

Line an 18 x 20 cm (7 x 8 inch) slab tin with baking paper. Put the Mars Bars and the 120 g (4¼ oz) of butter into a microwave-proof bowl. Microwave on high for about 2 minutes or until the Mars Bars melt. Remove the bowl, add the Rice Bubbles and stir them in. Pour the mixture into the prepared tray and, wearing food prep gloves or using clean, dry hands, press it out evenly. Refrigerate for 2 hours to set.

Put the chocolate and the 15 g (½ oz) of butter in a heatproof bowl and place over a saucepan of boiling water. Stir until the chocolate has melted. Pour over the Mars Bar slice and, using a spatula or palette knife, smooth the topping out so it is in an even layer. Return the tray to the fridge and leave for 2 hours for the topping to harden. Once completely set, un-mould the slice and cut into 1 x 3 cm (½ x 1¼ inch) pieces. Store in an airtight container.

PEANUT BUTTER DULCE DE LECHE

395 g (14 oz) tin condensed milk
100 g (3½ oz) smooth peanut butter

Puncture a small hole in the top of the tin of condensed milk (this will prevent it from exploding from pressure later). Put a small plate at the bottom of a deep saucepan and place the punctured tin on top. Fill the saucepan with enough water to reach about three-quarters of the way up the tin. Bring the water to a boil and continue to simmer for about 3 hours, keeping the water level topped up as it evaporates. After 3 hours, turn the heat off and leave the tin to sit in the water for an hour. Remove from the water and set aside to cool.

Open the tin and scoop out the condensed milk into a bowl. Add the peanut butter. Using a whisk, mix in 200 ml (7 fl oz) water a little at a time until you have a smooth texture. Cover and keep in the fridge until ready to use.

RASPBERRY SAUCE

500 g (1 lb 2 oz/4 cups) frozen raspberries
175 g caster (superfine) sugar

Add both ingredients to a small saucepan and cook over a medium heat, stirring occasionally for about 20 minutes or until a semi-thick consistency is achieved. You don't want to cook the sauce too long (this will create a jam – there should still be a little freshness about it).

BANANA FRITTERS

2 ripe bananas, peeled
kadaifi pastry
vegetable oil, for deep-frying
50 g (1¾ oz) icing (confectioners') sugar, mixed with ½ teaspoon ground cinnamon

Slice the bananas in half lengthways and then cut each half into two pieces. Spread the kadaifi pastry across the bench. Roll each piece of banana in the kadaifi at least four times, then cut and fold the pastry to make a nice banana parcel. Store in the fridge until ready to fry.

Fill a large heavy-based saucepan one-third full with vegetable oil and heat to 180°C (350°F) or until a cube of bread dropped into the oil turns golden in 15 seconds. Deep-fry the banana fritters in batches for about 1 minute, or until crisp and golden brown. Drain on paper towels and dust with cinnamon-infused icing sugar. Keep warm.

TO SERVE

Spoon some of the peanut butter dulce de leche on a plate, followed by a few teaspoons of raspberry sauce. Next, add a few tablespoons of potato chip praline to the plate followed by 4–5 pieces of Mars Bar slice. Place the banana fritter on one side and, on the other side, a scoop of doughnut ice cream. Stick a piece of candied bacon in the ice cream and serve.

Jow came up with this dish because he wanted to do breakfast as a dessert. It is basically a combination of a bowl of cornflakes with rice pudding and muesli. You can start preparing the rice for this dish a day ahead.

BREAKFAST

Serves at least 6

BURNT HONEY ICE CREAM
(The ice cream, cereal crumbs and milk crumbs can be made a day or two in advance.)
250 g (9 oz) Tasmanian leatherwood honey
12 egg yolks, lightly beaten
750 ml (26 fl oz/3 cups) milk
250 ml (9 fl oz/1 cup) thin (pouring) cream
2 tablespoons plain honey

Add the honey to a small saucepan over a high heat. Resist the urge to stir, just give the pan a little swirl and allow the heat to transform the honey into a caramel. When the mixture starts to caramelise (about 140°C/285°F on a sugar thermometer), carefully pour it into a bowl and add the egg yolks, whisking vigorously for about 5 minutes until light, airy and foamy.

Add the milk, cream and plain honey to a separate saucepan and bring to the boil. Slowly add to the yolk/honey mixture, whisking continuously until well combined. Remove from the heat, leave to cool then transfer to an ice-cream machine. Churn according to the manufacturer's instructions.

CEREAL CRUMBS
190 g (6¾ oz/6⅓ cups) cornflakes
190 g (6¾ oz) oatmeal
3¾ tablespoons maple syrup
1½ tablespoons caster (superfine) sugar
150 g (5½ oz) powdered milk
¼ teaspoon salt
250 g (9 oz) butter, melted

Preheat the oven to 135°C (260°F/Gas 1) and line a baking tray with baking paper. Put all the ingredients in a bowl, and wear food prep gloves to combine. Spread the mixture over the prepared tray and bake for 20–30 minutes until slightly brown and toasted. You might have to stir the mixture a few times so it browns evenly. Remove from the heat and leave to cool, then transfer to an airtight container.

MILK CRUMBS
80 g (2¾ oz) powdered milk
60 g (2¼ oz) plain (all-purpose) flour
1 tablespoon caster (superfine) sugar
¼ teaspoon salt
3 tablespoons cornflour (cornstarch)
40 g (1½ oz) butter, melted

Preheat the oven to 120°C (235°F/Gas ½) and line a baking tray with baking paper. In a bowl, combine 50 g (1¾ oz) of the powdered milk, the flour, sugar, salt and cornflour. Mix well then stir in the melted butter. Knead the mixture lightly then roughly flatten it out on the prepared tray. Bake for 20–30 minutes until dried, crumbly and lightly toasted. When done, toss through the remaining powdered milk. Store in an airtight container.

STICKY RICE

70 g (2½ oz) sticky rice (soaked overnight in water)
100 g (3½ oz) crème fraîche
100 ml (3½ fl oz) thin (pouring) cream
1½ tablespoons maple syrup
½ teaspoon ground cinnamon
1 teaspoon sugar

Drain the sticky rice and transfer it to a heatproof bowl. Place the bowl in a bamboo steamer over a saucepan of simmering water and steam for 15 minutes. At the same time, put the remaining ingredients in a small saucepan and warm them over a medium–low heat. When the rice is done, add it to the cream mixture and stir vigorously to combine well. The mixture should start to thicken and look a bit like risotto. Turn off the heat, and cover to keep warm.

POACHED CRANBERRIES

100 g (3½ oz) dried cranberries
200 ml (7 fl oz) sparkling wine
1 tablespoon caster (superfine) sugar
1 vanilla bean

Put the cranberries, wine and sugar in a saucepan. Split the vanilla bean in half and scrape out the seeds into the pan. You can also throw in the empty vanilla bean; just remember to discard it later. Bring to the boil over a medium heat and simmer for about 10 minutes, until most of the liquid has evaporated and the cranberries look plump.

TO SERVE

fresh strawberries, halved, quartered if large
fresh figs, cut into 1 cm (½ inch) wedges
fresh mango, cut into 2 cm (¾ inch) cubes

Add some warmed sticky rice into each of six serving bowls. Cover with some of the cereal mixture and then top with a few poached cranberries, strawberries, figs and mango and sprinkle with some milk crumbs. Lastly, add a scoop of burnt honey ice cream.

HONG HACK
Use any fruit in season for this recipe. With the burnt honey ice cream, we use leatherwood honey for its floral fragrance, but any honey you can find is fine. The recipe also calls for poached cranberries, but you could poach sultanas or dried apricots instead.

This dessert got its name because, at the time, all of the other desserts at Ms G's had a special name so we had to come up with something good for this one. 'Dirty' because there is a soil-type mixture on the plate and 'passion' because of the passionfruit curd hidden underneath the dirt. It's not rocket science.

DIRTY PASSION

Serves 4

COCONUT SORBET
125 g (4½ oz) caster (superfine) sugar
150 g (5½ oz) liquid glucose
230 ml (7¾ fl oz) coconut cream
300 ml (10½ fl oz) coconut water (the liquid inside a young coconut)

Using a hand-held blender, mix all the ingredients with a pinch of salt and 375 ml (13 fl oz/1½ cups) water in a bowl until well combined and the sugar and glucose dissolve. Transfer to an ice-cream machine and churn according to the manufacturer's instructions. Store in the freezer until ready to use.

DEHYDRATED CHOCOLATE MOUSSE
300 g (10½ oz) dark chocolate, chopped
5 egg yolks, lightly beaten
325 g (11½ oz) egg whites
½ teaspoon salt
100 g (3½ oz) caster (superfine) sugar

Preheat the oven to 70°C (150°F/Gas ¼). Line a baking tray with baking paper and set aside. Put the chocolate in a bowl and place over a saucepan of boiling water until it starts to melt. Using a rubber spatula, stir the chocolate until it has completely melted. Remove the bowl from the heat and leave for the chocolate to cool slightly (it should still be melted). Whisk in the egg yolks until well combined. In another bowl, whisk the egg whites with the salt and sugar until firm peaks form.

Add one-third of the egg whites to the chocolate mixture and gently fold it through. Follow with the rest of the egg whites. Be careful not to over-mix, as you want to retain as much air as possible. Spread out the mixture over the prepared tray and leave in the oven overnight or until the mixture is firm. Essentially, we are making a sort of chocolate meringue. Alternatively, if you own a dehydrator you can use this to dry the mixture out until it is firm. Store in an airtight container in the freezer.

PASSIONFRUIT CURD
7 egg yolks
2 eggs
250 g (9 oz) caster (superfine) sugar
160 ml (5¼ fl oz) passionfruit pulp (no seeds)
375 g (13 oz) cold unsalted butter, cut into 1.5 cm (⅝ inch) cubes

Put the egg yolks, eggs, sugar and passionfruit pulp in a bowl and whisk well. Set the bowl on top of a saucepan of boiling water and continue whisking. After a few minutes you will notice the mixture starting to thicken. Once it gets to a mayonnaise-like consistency, whisk in the butter (still over the heat) a few cubes at a time, waiting for each addition to melt before adding the next. Once all the butter has emulsified into the curd, take the bowl off the heat and cool it over a sink full of ice until it is cold. The curd should thicken as it cools down.

CHOCOLATE CRUMBS

140 g (5 oz/4⅔ cups) cornflakes, whizzed in a food processor to crumbs
400 g (14 oz) digestive biscuits, whizzed in a food processor to crumbs
250 g (9 oz) unsalted butter
3 tablespoons squid ink
200 g (7 oz/2 cups) almond meal
250 g (9 oz/2 cups) drinking chocolate powder
100 g (3½ oz) caster (superfine) sugar
220 g (7¾ oz/3⅓ cups) dried shredded coconut

Preheat the oven to 160°C (315°F/Gas 2–3) and line a baking tray with baking paper. Put the cornflakes into the bowl of a food processor, whizz to form crumbs and transfer to a large bowl. Do the same with the biscuits. Melt the butter in a saucepan over a medium heat, then whisk in the squid ink. Add all the other ingredients to the cornflake and biscuit crumbs except the shredded coconut. Wearing food prep gloves, mix everything well with your hands.

Add the squid ink butter to the mixture and continue to work the mixture until the crumbs become almost black. Finally, add the coconut and fold through. Spread the mixture over the prepared tray and bake for 2 minutes. Take the tray out of the oven, stir the mixture with a spoon then bake for another 2 minutes. Cool.

THE REST

Choose a combination of seasonal fresh tropical fruit such as lychees, mangoes, golden kiwifruit or dragonfruit. Cut into bite-sized pieces.

TO SERVE

Spoon 2 tablespoons of passionfruit curd into each of four bowls and top with some pieces of fruit. Cover the mixture with some chocolate crumbs then top with a few shards of chocolate mousse. Lastly, add a scoop of coconut sorbet on top.

I was once asked to create a dessert challenge for *MasterChef Australia* contestants. The mystery ingredient turned out to be lemons, so I came up with this. Immediately after the show, we had queues of people lined up outside the restaurant just to try it. All of the components can be made in advance, making it a good dinner party assembly dessert.

LEMON TART

Serves 6

LEMON GRANITA
350 ml (12 fl oz) lemon juice
zest of 3 lemons
300 g (10½ oz) caster (superfine) sugar
150 ml (5 fl oz) soda water

Put all the ingredients in a bowl with 670 ml (23 fl oz/2⅔ cups) water and whisk until the sugar dissolves. Pour the mixture into a shallow tray or plastic container and freeze until ice crystals form. Remove from the freezer, mix the crystals around with a fork, then return to the freezer. Repeat this process another three or four times.

LEMON CURD
5 large egg yolks
2 whole eggs
250 g (9 oz) caster (superfine) sugar
150 ml (5 fl oz) lemon juice
zest of 3 lemons
375 g (13 oz) cold butter, diced into cubes

Put the egg yolks, whole eggs and sugar in a bowl and whisk well. Place the bowl on top of a saucepan of boiling water and continue whisking. Add the lemon juice and zest and continue to whisk. After a few minutes you will notice the mixture starting to thicken to a mayonnaise-like consistency. Whisk in the butter (still over the heat) a few cubes at a time, waiting for each addition to melt before adding the next. Once all the butter has been added and emulsified into the curd, take the bowl off the heat and sit it over a sink full of ice until it is cold. The curd should thicken as it cools down.

STREUSEL
150 g (5½ oz) digestive biscuits
165 g (5¾ oz) butter, softened
150 g (5½ oz/⅔ cup) caster (superfine) sugar
½ teaspoon salt
150 g (5½ oz/1 cup) plain (all-purpose) flour
½ teaspoon baking powder

Preheat the oven to 160°C (315°F/Gas 2–3) and line a baking tray with baking paper. Put the biscuits into the bowl of a food processor and blitz to create an even crumb. Transfer to a bowl. In a separate bowl, add the butter, sugar and salt and whisk, using electric hand-beaters, until light and fluffy.

Add the flour and baking powder to the digestive biscuits and mix together. Combine the dry ingredients with the butter mixture and mix lightly until crumbly. Be careful not to over-mix as you want to leave some air in the mixture. Spoon the mixture onto the prepared tray and bake for 10 minutes or until golden.

MASCARPONE SORBET
500 g (1 lb 2 oz) mascarpone cheese
600 ml (21 fl oz) sugar syrup (Essentials, page 240)
125 ml (4 fl oz/½ cup) lemon juice

In a bowl, whisk all the ingredients together until combined. Transfer to an ice-cream machine and churn according to the manufacturer's instructions.

CANDIED LEMON
2 lemons
maple syrup

Using a vegetable peeler, carefully remove the zest of the lemons in strips, making sure you don't take off any bitter white pith. Put the strips in a saucepan with just enough maple syrup to cover them and bring the syrup to the boil. As soon as it reaches boiling point, take the pan off the heat and leave the zest to cool in the syrup.

TO SERVE

Spoon 2 tablespoons of lemon curd into each of six dessert glasses or bowls, then top with 2 tablespoons of the streusel and a scoop of mascarpone sorbet. Top with a few candied lemon peel strips and cover the whole thing in lemon granita.

MY TOP 10 WORLD CUISINES

Australia is a good place for food-loving people. While there is an abundance of meat and three veg options – food I often regard as being one-dimensional – you can also be exposed to a diverse range of cuisines that employ different seasonings to bring out the flavour of ingredients. When you start to understand that using a little bit of sugar balances salty food, or you can appreciate the value of how herbs, fish sauce, even MSG can take your palate to places it's never been before... that's really 'getting' flavour.

I want to clarify something. I like big flavour, yes. But I also appreciate simple food with single, clear flavours. A piece of perfect sashimi, for example – there's nothing better. I also love things like a really beautiful piece of cured ham, or the brightness and acidity of a good dill pickle.

I also like compiling lists. It's sort of like sport for me. My top 10 ramens in Sydney, favourite albums, death row meals. I think it's a really good way of getting to know what someone is about. So I couldn't really write a book without sharing one top 10 list with you which is, of course, about the food I like.

1. CHINESE

Of all the cuisines that do roasted meats, the Chinese have perfected it – roast duck, suckling pig, pork belly, even their steamed chicken (a dish commonly found in Chinese BBQ houses). But that's not where it stops. From refined and elegant Cantonese to unapologetically spicy Sichuan cuisine, rustic handmade noodles and dumplings from the north to the fresh and salted chilli heat of Hunan – there's such diversity in one continent. It's the techniques and flavours that make Chinese food complex and delicious. An equal first place alongside Vietnamese and Japanese for me.

1. VIETNAMESE

Probably a nod to nostalgia, but it's *my* list (and I'll write it if I want to). For me, Vietnamese food is in equal first with Chinese food. It's about the balance of fresh herbs, pungent fermented ingredients, bright vinegary notes and meat every way you can think of. It's a lot like Thai, but a little more pared back, plus the greater use of herbs adds more fragance and grace.

1. JAPANESE

The Japanese put so much emphasis on attention to detail. They *must* do the very best version of everything. Their obsession with perfection is amazing. Ramen, sushi, sashimi – these dishes are in many ways so simple, and yet that perfection is what makes them complex to master.

2. FRENCH

The foundations of my training as a chef began with French cuisine. But those French influences go way back in my food memory to Vietnam, when the Vietnamese adopted French cuisine into their repertoire. I love charcuterie (something I grew up eating thanks to my grandmother), and, of course, the French were the founders of great pastry and bread.

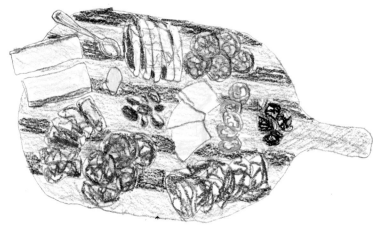

3. SINGAPOREAN

Black pepper crab, chilli crab, Hainanese chicken rice – anything sold in those hawker-style food courts is good... *char kway teow*, satay. And the people? They're so food-obsessed that you can access amazing eats at any time of the day. The whole nation is a serious bunch of eaters.

4. LAOTIAN

It's like Thai food, but stinkier! Fermented fish and crab hit places on your palate you've probably never reached before. My mum used to take us to eat in Fairfield in Sydney's west, where there is a big Laotian community. That's where I ate my first plate of grilled tongue. I love larb, fertilised duck eggs and Lao sausages.

5. THAI

Thai is not higher on my list because I simply can't eat it every day and because it's become so bastardised around the world. Thai food has, however, been a big influence on developing my palate and really opened my eyes to those big, bold flavours – green papaya salad, grilled pork neck, sticky rice.

6. SPANISH

Jamón, jamón, jamón and the simplicity of their seafood dishes. One of my most memorable meals was actually the night before I went to elBulli. I went to a place called Raffa's. He has all this seafood on display and just cooks it *a la plancha*. I remember sucking out the heads of these incredible prawns and they remain some of the sweetest prawns I've ever eaten. The Spanish see beauty in simplicity.

7. AMERICAN

Hamburgers, hotdogs, fried chicken, buffalo wings, American pit-style BBQ. I didn't really appreciate it until I went there. If there is one thing Americans do well, it's junk food. They take it to the next level. It may seem like junk here... but there it's just food. They've mastered the art of low and slow cooking. Even weirder, I found a new respect for bologna when I visited Tennessee (of all places).

8. KOREAN

Kimchi is one of the greatest culinary discoveries in the world. It's up there with *jamón*, sashimi, dim sum. It all comes back to that Thai, Lao, Viet thing about fermentation, fishiness, and therefore umami. I did *tae kwon do* lessons when I was a kid and I remember there was a graduation celebration where we ate *chap chae* (potato noodles), Korean sushi and all the sides. When it comes to barbecue, the Koreans were onto beef short ribs long before the rest of us. The food is punchy and pungent, but spiked with acidity.

9. INDONESIAN

My wife would kill me if this wasn't in my top 10 as she is from Jakarta. And if she wasn't successful, I'm fairly sure my mother-in-law would finish the job. I didn't really know about Indonesian food until I met Rara. I love the rich, curry-like braised dishes of Padang cuisine, and Balinese cuisine for the fresh grilled seafood and *babi guling* (suckling pig). Sunda cuisine is all about fresh herbs and deep-fried offal.

10. ITALIAN

I'm funny about Italian. If it's executed really well, it's awesome. If it isn't... forgeddaboudit. The Italians do some of the world's best charcuterie, and I love the simplicity of Italian flavours. I'm also a bit of a tiramisu tragic. That's my one exception: it could be a shitty one from the supermarket, or a perfect example of authenticity, I don't care, I'm eating it.

CHAPTER THREE

TACOS AND THE EL LOCO STORY

I never thought I'd open a Mexican restaurant (or even a vaguely Mexican restaurant), but that's what happens when you work with someone like Justin Hemmes. His ideas are often larger than most people can get their heads around, but his knack for predicting what will work continues to challenge me (in a good way). In the midst of the craziness that was opening Ms G's (22 days straight on practically zero sleep), Justin sat me down and said, 'I just bought this pub in Surry Hills and I want to open a Mexican place there. I want you to run it.'

'OK... I don't know anything about Mexican food... '

Justin explained to me that he knew I could learn and execute whatever I set my mind to and then nail it. I'm lucky that Justin and I seem to speak the same language when it comes to imagining the potential of a space or an idea. As a chef, when someone asks you to do something like this, it's at once a completely daunting prospect and an absolutely mind-blowing opportunity. I thought to myself, 'This is an opportunity that probably doesn't come up very often. Why wouldn't you take it?' So the next day, I called him back and said: 'I'll do it.'

We went down to The Excelsior (the pub he'd just bought) to have a look... it was a shithole. I said to Justin: 'I still don't know anything about Mexican food.' And he asked me where I wanted to go to figure it out.

Justin had just been to Coachella for four days and I caught up with him in LA to get down to the business of research. We jumped in this ridiculously huge Escalade and basically stalked every single taco truck. I ate about 40 tacos that night. I remember thinking that this was the first time I'd really tasted proper tacos.

I now regard Mexican food and Vietnamese food to be quite similar – both cuisines are really fresh, there are a lot of grilled foods, the salsas are clean, and they both have beautiful acidic dressings. In both Mexico and Vietnam chopped coriander and onions are used to cut the richness of meat, while herbs aid in balance and aroma.

But the trip wasn't all about seeking authentic Mexican food. Korean–American chef Roy Choi's food truck, Kogi, was a revelation. It combined Korean ideas and treatments and applied them to tacos. Extra dimensions of flavour came through marinades and dressings and the mix of cultures created a really potent flavour profile. This approach planted a seed in my mind about how I would eventually approach this menu.

From the start, I knew I couldn't do a traditional Mexican at El Loco. Firstly, it's not my background and secondly, I wanted to stamp my own style on it.

When I arrived in Mexico, my friend Laura Londoño (with whom I worked at Lotus) arranged for a local friend of hers to pick me up and show me around.

I met up with him every day and he'd take me to different places that were known for their specialities:

Carnitas: literally, the whole pig inside a tortilla. There's a little bit of everything, from crackling, to tripe, tongue, ear... and just a bit of salsa verde to cut through the fattiness.

Tacos al pastor: show the influence of Middle Eastern food in Mexico. It's like a doner kebab with grilled pork and pineapple.

Cochinita pibil: a traditional dish of pork marinated then slow-braised in bitter orange and served with habañero salsa.

When we got back to Sydney, I had a clear idea of what I wanted to do with the menu for El Loco. Like Kogi, which took the best elements of Korean cuisine and blended them with Mexican to create its own unique style, El Loco would be about layering Vietnamese (and other Asian) flavour profiles in a complementary way with Mexican ones. This is really evident in the salad component of the tacos. In Mexico, salads are not usually dressed: the taco starts with the meat on the bottom, then salad greens, then a salsa on top. By dressing the salad with condiments like fish sauce, sesame oil, soy, ginger, it not only added the Asian element, but another dimension of flavour.

When Justin and I returned to Sydney, we had four days to launch El Loco and so the food had to be simple to prepare, super tasty and easy to assemble. We gave away about 3,000 free tacos on opening night, and even had a donkey wearing a sombrero, just, you know, hanging out.

The whole point of El Loco is that you can go there and have a good time. If you want to drink and just have a snack, you can. If you want a full-on feast and then stay for a drink, you can do that too. Anything goes, so long as it's fun.

TACOS

The food at El Loco isn't Mexican. Or at least, it isn't authentic. It's more of a blend of textures and flavours that make sense to me. El Loco takes the ideals of Mexican cuisine – freshness, spice, rich flavours, contrast – and mixes them with complementary flavour profiles in Asian food. I'd like to think the result is the kind of food you want to inhale with one hand, while holding a margarita in the other.

LEMONGRASS BEEF TACO

Makes 10

SALSA VERDE
500 g (1 lb 2 oz) fresh tomatillos
1 red onion
½ avocado
2 jalapeño peppers
2 bunches coriander (cilantro)
juice of 2 limes

Using the pulse action, blend all the ingredients in a food processor to a salsa-like consistency. You still want a little texture, so be careful not to over-blend it. Season with salt.

MARINADE
100 g (3½ oz) caster (superfine) sugar
1 spring onion (scallion), finely chopped
100 ml (3½ fl oz) fish sauce
100 ml (3½ fl oz) Knorr Liquid Seasoning
3 garlic cloves, finely chopped

Whisk all the ingredients together in a bowl until the sugar dissolves.

FOR THE MEAT
700 g (1 lb 9 oz) piece of grain-fed scotch fillet, rump or sirloin
vegetable oil, for frying
10 x 12 cm (4 x 4½ inch) white corn tortillas

Cut the beef into 5 mm x 3 cm (¼ x 1¼ inch) strips. Transfer to a bowl and pour the marinade in. Mix everything with clean hands until combined, then leave for at least 2 hours for the beef to marinate.

Put two frying pans on the stove. Add a little oil to the first pan over a medium–high heat and fry the beef in batches. Don't overcrowd the pan, as you want the beef to caramelise. Stir every now and then as the marinade has lots of sugar in it and it will burn if left to sit. Cook for 3–4 minutes until the beef is done, then set aside and keep warm.

Don't add oil to the second pan. Instead, heat over a medium heat, warm the tortillas one or two at a time until they soften and the edges start to char slightly. Don't cook them too long or they will completely dry out and go hard. Keep them warm in a folded tea towel (dish towel) until ready to use.

SALAD DRESSING
2½ tablespoons light soy sauce
2½ tablespoons sugar
2½ tablespoons rice wine vinegar
2½ tablespoons grapeseed oil
1¼ tablespoons sesame oil

Whisk all the ingredients with 2½ tablespoons water in a bowl until the sugar dissolves.

FOR THE SALAD
150 g (5½ oz) Chinese cabbage (wong bok), thinly sliced
1 bunch coriander (cilantro), roughly chopped, including stems
5 spring onions (scallions), finely chopped

Combine the cabbage, coriander and spring onions in a bowl. Gradually add the salad dressing until you reach an amount you're happy with. Mix, taste and add more dressing if needed.

TO SERVE
200 g (7 oz) haloumi cheese

Place the tortillas on a large serving plate. Divide the cooked beef between the 10 tortillas, then add some cabbage salad, followed by a spoonful of salsa verde. Using a microplane, grate some haloumi cheese all over the top. Serve immediately.

HONG HACK
Tomatillos are available from farmers' markets when in season. Substitute with green (unripe) tomatoes.

I knew I wanted to put offal tacos on the menu, but I also knew nobody would order them. These were the best tacos I ate in Mexico and the United States and I wanted to share the beauty of what really good offal could be... It can be glorious! Here's what I discovered at El Loco: if you pair offal with an awesome salsa, anyone is going to eat it.

When we wrote the menu, we thought, 'How can we do this? How can we encourage people to be adventurous and try something different?' The rule was that staff was not allowed – under any circumstances – to tell people what was in the secret taco until after they'd finished eating it. And it worked. I'm super-happy that a lot of people have the balls to order it knowing the 'secret' ingredient was probably going to include something they might not ordinarily order. The rule is still in place today and most who try it feel a sense of achievement that they've gone there.

SECRET TACO

Makes 10

SWEET CORN SALSA
2 large ripe tomatoes, coarsely chopped
200 g (7 oz) fresh tomatillos, coarsely chopped
½ red onion, coarsely chopped
1 bunch coriander (cilantro), coarsely chopped
1 jalapeño pepper, seeded, coarsely chopped
2 garlic cloves
juice of 2 limes
kernels of 2 cobs of fresh sweet corn

Put all the ingredients except the sweet corn in a food processor and blend to a salsa consistency (not too smooth). Season to taste with salt then add the sweet corn.

SALAD DRESSING
2½ tablespoons light soy sauce
2½ tablespoons sugar
2½ tablespoons rice wine vinegar
2½ tablespoons grapeseed oil
1¼ tablespoons sesame oil

Whisk all the ingredients with 2½ tablespoons water in a bowl until the sugar dissolves.

CHIPOTLE MAYONNAISE
100 g (3½ oz) Chipotle Peppers In Adobo Sauce
700 g (1 lb 9 oz) Japanese mayonnaise

Put the chipotles into the bowl of a food processor and process until a smooth paste forms. Whisk this with the mayonnaise in a bowl, then transfer to a squeezie bottle. Store in the fridge until needed.

THE REST
10 tortillas
150 g (5½ oz) Chinese cabbage (wong bok), shredded
1 bunch coriander (cilantro), roughly chopped, including stems
5 spring onions (scallions), finely chopped

To warm the tortillas, put one or two at a time in a dry (don't add any oil) frying pan over a medium heat. Leave until they soften and the edges start to slightly char. Don't cook them too long or they will completely dry out. Keep them soft and warm in a folded tea towel (dish towel) until ready to use.

Combine the cabbage, coriander and spring onions in a small bowl. Add the salad dressing a little at a time, mixing well.

Put the tortillas on a large serving plate and top each with your chosen offal (pages 120–1). Add some cabbage salad, followed by a spoonful of sweet corn salsa and a squiggle of chipotle mayonnaise.

OFFAL!

My favourite tacos were always the offal tacos. I grew up eating offal – tripe, tongue, pork stomach – and I love the stuff. Mexicans value offal the way Asians do. That is, if you prepare and cook it right, it's super tasty. Using each and every part of the animal – from the T-bone to the testicles – is also a sign of respect. Like many cuisines around the world, Mexican and Vietnamese cuisines were born from poverty, during times and circumstances when nobody could afford to waste anything edible. Today, in Mexico, one of the most common dishes I noticed on offer – served everywhere from stand-up taquerias to cantinas – is slow-cooked ox tripe and beef intestines. You order, they grab it from a large copper pot, chop it, put it on the plancha to crisp and caramelise and then put it on a taco.

CHICKEN HEARTS

Cut hearts in half and marinate in a mixture of grated garlic, grated ginger, sugar, soy sauce and sesame oil for about 2 hours. Cook in a hot frying pan or plancha until well done for about 4 minutes.

CHICKEN LIVERS

Wash thoroughly under running water to remove excess blood. Trim and discard any ducts or sinew and cut into 2 cm (¾ inch) pieces. Marinate in the same mixture as for the chicken hearts and pan-fry over a high heat. I like mine still pink in the middle, which takes about 3 minutes.

OX/PORK TONGUE

Braise in Chinese masterstock (Essentials, page 234) for 4–5 hours until soft. Remove and cool slightly before peeling off the tough outer layer. Refrigerate until firm then dice into 1 cm (½ inch) pieces. Cook on a plancha or hot frying pan until crispy and caramelised.

HONEYCOMB TRIPE

Blanch tripe in boiling water and then braise for about 4 hours in Chinese masterstock (Essentials, page 234). Remove from the stock and refrigerate. Once cold, dice the tripe into 1 cm (½ inch) cubes and cook on a plancha or in a frying pan until crispy and caramelised.

LAMB'S BRAINS

Rinse well then poach in salted water with a little garlic, ginger and onion for 5 minutes, or until cooked and firm. Drain and cut into 3 cm (1¼ inch) cubes. Follow the classic crumbing technique of dusting with plain (all-purpose) flour, dipping in beaten egg and then coating in dry breadcrumbs. Deep-fry until golden brown then season with salt.

PORK UTERUS OR STOMACH

Braise in Chinese masterstock (Essentials, page 234) for about 2 hours. Remove and refrigerate. Once cold, cut into 1 cm (½ inch) pieces and fry in a hot frying pan or plancha until caramelised and crispy.

TESTICLES OF BEEF/LAMB/PORK

Remove each testicle from its sack and separate the outer membrane using a knife (much like you remove the skin of a fish fillet). Cut into 1 cm (½ inch) cubes and leave to marinate in the fridge in a mixture of raw sugar, fish sauce and grated ginger for at least 2 hours. Cook in a hot frying pan or plancha until well done.

OX/PORK/LAMB HEARTS

Cut straight through the middle of the heart to butterfly it. Remove all large arteries and vessels with a sharp knife. Cook it sous-vide in a vacuum-sealed bag with a mixture of soy sauce, sesame oil, sugar, grated garlic and salt for 12 hours. Chill in iced water, then cut into 1 cm (½ inch) cubes. Fry the hearts in a frying pan or plancha over a high heat for about 4 minutes or until well done. If you don't have a sous-vide set-up at home, prepare the hearts up to that step then braise them in the oven in a covered ovenproof saucepan for 6–8 hours at 82°C (180°F/Gas ½). Finish it the same way as the sous-vide method above.

LAMB/VEAL SWEETBREADS

Wash thoroughly and blanch in salted boiling water with a little garlic, ginger and onion until cooked and firm (4 minutes for lamb, 8 for veal). Drain and cool slightly, then carefully peel away and discard the outer membrane. Cut into 3 cm (1¼ inch) pieces and follow the classic crumbing technique of dusting with plain (all-purpose) flour, dipping in beaten egg and coating with dry breadcrumbs. Deep-fry until golden brown then season with salt.

Hotdogs are probably one of my favourite things to eat – ever. I might even love them more than burgers.

The most important thing for me when it comes to a hotdog is sausage overhang. The sausage absolutely must be longer than the bun… because while people might get sick of eating the bun, nobody ever leaves the dog behind. Another important hotdog element is the 'snap' you get when you bite into the skin of the sausage. We worked with our smallgoods maker on all kinds of combinations of casings and meats but it comes down, for us, to a Vienna-style sausage in a beef casing. They make 2,000 of them each week just for us.

The El Loco dog is a hotdog on steroids. Because the restaurant came together in literally a matter of days, we looked at the other condiments we had created for the restaurant: pico de gallo and jalapeños, being a couple of them. These ingredients not only give the dish its Mexican feel, but also add acidity and brightness. Next, a hotdog needs mustard and relish. Our answer to that is a blend of the two: a honey mustard combined with blended gherkins for that familiar flavour, while Japanese mayo is another (subjective, but) great thing to have in there too. Rather than chunky tasty cheese, we found haloumi was easy to microplane, giving the hotdog an almost halo of cheese on top. We never thought it would become the best-selling item on the menu, but it just goes to show how much of a crowd-pleaser a hotdog can be.

EL LOCO HOTDOG

Serves 6

PICO DE GALLO
4 large ripe tomatoes, seeded, very finely chopped
½ red onion, very finely chopped
1 bunch coriander (cilantro), very finely chopped
1 jalapeño pepper, very finely chopped
2 garlic cloves, very finely chopped

MUSTARD RELISH
2 large gherkins (pickles)
150 g (5½ oz) American mustard
50 g (1¾ oz) honey

THE REST
vegetable oil, for frying
6 good-quality German frankfurts (dogs)
6 store-bought hotdog buns
150 g (5½ oz) pickled jalapeño peppers, sliced
Japanese mayonnaise (Kenko brand)
200 g (7 oz) haloumi cheese

Start with the pico de gallo. Mix all the ingredients together and season with salt to taste. Refrigerate until ready to use.

For the mustard relish, pulse the pickles in a food processor until they've become small cubes. Add the mustard and honey and blend to combine. Decant into a squeezie bottle and set aside in the fridge.

To cook the frankfurts, heat a little oil in a frying pan over a medium heat and fry the dogs until heated through and the casings are nicely caramelised.

Meanwhile, line a bamboo steamer with baking paper. Put the buns inside, place over a saucepan of simmering water and steam for 30 seconds. Once this is done, halve the buns lengthways and place the frankfurt inside. Insert a few pickled jalapeño slices under the dog and put more on top. Spoon a liberal layer of pico de gallo over this, covering most of the frankfurt. Next, squiggle over some mustard relish and Japanese mayonnaise. Using a microplane, liberally grate haloumi cheese all over the top. Serve immediately.

CHAPTER FOUR
MR WONG

After the success of Ms G's and El Loco, Justin came back to talk about opening a Chinese restaurant in the middle of Sydney's CBD. Tank was a hugely popular nightclub that opened in 2001. Justin's vision was to transform the vast subterranean space into a huge Chinese restaurant, complete with bronzed, roasted ducks hanging in the window and dim sum. With such a huge task on my hands, I wanted Jow to be the head chef.

As well as his passion for Chinese cuisine, Jow had an understanding of how we'd make the food distinct. While it's fair to say I've probably eaten at every decent Chinese restaurant in Sydney, neither Jow nor I had any formal culinary training in Chinese cuisine. Chinese food is both subtle and complex. It requires very specific knowledge and a set of techniques in order to pull it off, as well as skills and recipes passed down through the generations.

I'll admit that research trips are pretty cool, but they are also a lot of hard work. Every mealtime and in between mealtimes is spent eating, writing notes and more eating. At different times, Jow and I travelled to Hong Kong and ate everywhere from street food stalls in Wan Chai to Michelin-starred places like Tim's Kitchen, Lung King Heen and Lei Garden.

The brief for Mr Wong was to be able to offer everything from dim sum to roast duck... all the classic dishes. We started testing and researching dishes, working out how we'd apply our own style to them, while maintaining a sense of authenticity.

We also needed a dim sum chef. Making great dumplings is considered an art form. You can't just start making them – you train for twice as many years as a chef would train and then you keep on training. We were super lucky that Eric Koh, a talented dim sum chef who had worked at Hakkasan and Yauatcha in London, was interested in working with us because his family live in Singapore (and Australia is a lot closer than London).

When he came over to do a tasting, I hadn't eaten dim sim of that quality anywhere outside of Hong Kong. I knew we had to get him because he'd blow every other yum cha restaurant out of the water.

Similarly, mastering the art of a Chinese BBQ is a whole different ball game. We hired Jack Lam from Hong Kong. His mate, our stir-fry chef, told us he was coming to Sydney to look for work. He'd only been doing Chinese BBQ for two years (which is nothing, as Chinese BBQ chefs can spend decades dedicated to just this one art), which was perfect because he was open to our ideas on tweaking techniques and flavours.

My one beef with a lot of Chinese food is produce. There are a lot of dishes that could be lighter, fresher and more vibrant if they only used better produce and relied less on starches. When I was growing up and my mum ran her first Vietnamese restaurant, she picked up the attention of food critics because she took the basics of Vietnamese cuisine and combined it with the best produce she could afford. She also gave the dishes her own signature. It's funny that after all my years in fine dining I should end up doing exactly what I'd been exposed to from the very start.

So Mr Wong's menu is a mixture of classics (with a twist) and things I thought were missing, like lighter dishes, salads, raw dishes and a few really good desserts.

The menu at Mr Wong's features about 70 items, excluding specials. It took about five months to test everything, but the feedback from the brains trust about dishes like sweet and sour pork hock, Lo Hun–style baby vegetables and deep-fried ice cream was a collective thumbs-up.

Everything aside from the salt and pepper squid, that is. That really stumped me. I could make it work in small batches, but there was something about the batter that didn't quite come together for me. I tried every conceivable combination of techniques, batter recipes and flours, but at 1 am on the morning of the first soft launch, I was lost. It was a nightmare. Then, I thought about how consistently perfect my mum's salt and pepper squid was at her restaurant. I called her and she gave me her recipe, which of course worked like magic. Thanks Mum.

Everything about Mr Wong is big. It seats 240 people and there are 40 chefs on the roster. That we have managed to pull it off still blows my mind a little. And to think, after I'd finally reached the point where I realised success meant a full restaurant, the awards became the icing on the cake: Mr Wong was awarded Best New Restaurant by both *Gourmet Traveller* and the *Good Food Guide* in 2012. I even managed a nomination for *Good Food Guide* Chef of the Year. Crazy.

I love steak tartare because to make a really good one – it's all about the seasoning. It has to be almost too tasty, in order to make it the dish it is. Salty, sour, sweet, you can basically use steak tartare as a vehicle to carry the flavours of any cuisine you like: it's just about applying the elemental flavours of that cuisine and topping it with a raw egg yolk.

Sichuan food has lots of chilli oil, Sichuan pepper, dried roasted chillies, while a Vietnamese version might feature plenty of fresh, mixed herbs like coriander (cilantro), Vietnamese mint, lemongrass and, of course, fish sauce. I've also played with Thai (lime leaf, roasted rice, lime juice, chilli, fish sauce) and Mexican (dried chipotle, coriander, served with tortilla chips) versions of this dish.

To make Sichuan steak tartare, it's important you use the best-quality piece of beef you can afford. I use tri-tip (triangular in shape, cut from the bottom of the sirloin) because it has a good texture and chew, rather than using fillet, which is a bit too soft. To appreciate the texture and quality of the beef, it must be chopped by hand, regardless of which cut you choose.

SICHUAN STEAK TARTARE

Serves 6

DRESSING

1¼ tablespoons rice wine vinegar
1¼ tablespoons sugar syrup (Essentials, page 240)
2½ tablespoons Chinkiang black vinegar
2½ tablespoons mirin
150 ml (5 fl oz light soy sauce)
½ teaspoon finely grated garlic
2 teaspoons finely grated ginger

Whisk all the ingredients together in a bowl. Set aside.

BEEF TARTARE BASE

400 g (14 oz) piece of good-quality beef tri-tip
4 spring onions (scallions), thinly sliced
4 tablespoons Lao Gan Ma chilli oil

Remove all visible sinew from the beef with a sharp knife, then cut into very small 4 x 4 mm (¼ x ¼ inch) cubes. Put in a bowl and add the spring onions, chilli oil and 160 ml (5¼ fl oz) of the dressing. Combine everything with clean hands until the ingredients are nicely mixed together. Cover and set aside.

THE REST

cassava crackers
vegetable oil, for frying
4 tablespoons fried garlic chips (Essentials, page 242)
1 small handful of baby coriander (cilantro) leaves, to garnish
2 telegraph (long) cucumbers, sliced diagonally

Fry the cassava crackers in oil according to the packet instructions.

Divide the tartare mixture among six plates. Sprinkle each plate with some fried garlic chips and top with some baby coriander. Serve immediately, with the fried cassava crackers and cucumber slices on the side.

HONG HACK
Cassava crackers are available at most Asian grocery stores, but if you can't find them, prawn crackers or whole deep-fried wonton skins work well, too.

This was the first raw dish I came up with for Mr Wong that showcased Chinese flavours. I had in my head, the idea of surf and turf, which eventually morphed into lap cheong sausage and scallops. The sweetness in both lap cheong and the scallops works really well here, while the wood ear fungus and roasted rice pellets bring texture to the dish.

SASHIMI of SEA SCALLOPS, LAP CHEONG and WOOD EAR FUNGUS

Serves 4

DRESSING
2½ tablespoons sesame oil
3¼ tablespoons shiro-dashi
3¼ tablespoons light soy sauce
100 ml (3½ fl oz) sugar syrup (Essentials, page 240)
100 ml (3½ fl oz) ginger oil (Essentials, page 238)
1 tablespoon lemon juice

Whisk all the ingredients together in a bowl. Set aside.

THE REST
16 sashimi-grade scallops, roe and skirts removed
1 lap cheong (Chinese sausage), sliced into 2 mm (¹⁄₁₆ inch) rounds
2 spring onions (scallions), thinly sliced into rounds
100 g (3½ oz) fresh wood ear mushrooms
1 tablespoon tsubu arare (roasted rice pellets), to garnish

Thinly slice each scallop into 2 or 3 rounds, depending on how thick they are. Divide among four plates, not overlapping. Top each piece of scallop with a slice of lap cheong. Sprinkle with spring onions and spread a few wood ear mushrooms around each plate.

Whisk the dressing and spoon generously over each dish. Garnish with some roasted rice pellets to serve.

The Chinese don't really eat raw chrysanthemum leaves, but I noticed when I tried them uncooked that they add fragrance to any dish they are served with. The nashi pear and red vinegar also enhance the sweetness of the crabmeat. I believe snow crab to be the best eating crab in the world – super sweet and with great texture.

SALAD of SNOW CRAB, CHRYSANTHEMUM LEAVES, NASHI PEAR and GINGER

Serves 4

VINAIGRETTE
1½ tablespoons sugar syrup (Essentials, page 240)
3¼ tablespoons shiro-dashi
3¼ tablespoons white soy sauce
100 ml (3½ fl oz) Chinese red vinegar
125 ml (4 fl oz/½ cup) ginger oil (Essentials, page 238)

Whisk all the vinaigrette ingredients together in a bowl until well combined. Set aside.

THE REST
4 cm (1½ inch) piece young ginger, peeled and finely julienned
1 nashi pear, cored, cut into matchsticks, about 5 mm (¼ inch) thick
400 g (14 oz) snow crab meat, picked over
1 bunch chrysanthemum (tong ho), leaves picked
1 tablespoon trout roe, to garnish

Put the julienned ginger in a bowl of cold water for 20 minutes. In a separate bowl, add the nashi pear, crabmeat, chrysanthemum leaves and drained ginger. Mix gently but thoroughly, then add about 200 ml (7 fl oz) of the vinaigrette. Mix again, taking care not to bruise the chrysanthemum leaves. Serve on a platter or divide among four plates, garnished with trout roe.

When I opened Mr Wong, I knew I wanted jellyfish on the menu. This really is a dish about texture. Jellyfish doesn't have a lot of flavour, but it absorbs other flavours nicely. Again, the pig's ears have no strong flavour, but they bring a textural, crunchy cartilage-y and gelatinous element to the dish. The jellyfish takes some time to desalinate and prepare (Essentials, page 245), but once you've done this, the rest is pretty straightforward.

POACHED CHICKEN, JELLYFISH and **PIG'S EAR SALAD**

Serves 5, or 12 as part of a banquet

CHICKEN AND PIG'S EARS

1.3 kg (3 lb) whole chicken
6 litres (210 fl oz/24 cups) Chinese masterstock (Essentials, page 234)
8 pig's ears

Season the chicken well, inside and out, with salt and pepper. Bring the masterstock to the boil in a large stockpot, then add the chicken. When the masterstock has returned to the boil, simmer for 10 minutes, then remove from the heat and cover with a lid. Leave the chicken to steep for 4 hours, then remove it from the liquid. When cool enough to handle, remove the skin and shred the meat. Reserve the bones and skin to nibble on.

For the pig's ears, use a blowtorch (or gas barbecue lighter) to singe off all visible hairs. Bring the masterstock back up to the boil, add the ears and simmer them for no more than 1 hour. Transfer to a plate and cool in the fridge. When completely cold, slice thinly into fine strips.

THE DRESSING

2½ tablespoons sugar syrup (Essentials, page 240)
100 ml (3½ fl oz) sesame oil
100 ml (3½ fl oz) Chinese red vinegar
100 ml (3½ fl oz) soy sauce

Whisk all the ingredients with 2½ tablespoons water in a bowl until the sugar dissolves.

THE SALAD

1 telegraph (long) cucumber, seeded, sliced into thin batons
150 g (5½ oz) compressed celery (Essentials, page 245), cut into 2 mm (¹⁄₁₆ inch) batons
2 bunches coriander (cilantro), leaves only
5 spring onions (scallions), julienned
4 cm (1½ inch) piece young ginger, cut into thin matchsticks

THE REST

250 g (9 oz) marinated jellyfish (Essentials, page 245), thinly sliced
sesame seeds, garnish

To assemble, combine all the salad ingredients in a bowl. Add the chicken, pig's ears, jellyfish and half the dressing (be sure to whisk this before pouring it in). Mix everything well with clean hands. Taste, and add more dressing if needed. Divide among five plates, or arrange in one large serving bowl for a banquet. Garnish with sesame seeds before serving.

DRUNKEN
CHICKEN

The menu we created at Mr Wong is a mixture of classics, and dishes that feature our spin on other classic Chinese dishes. Drunken chicken, which originated in southern China, is another take on a classic at Mr Wong. A bit of French culinary training came into play here, as we decided to make a ballotine out of the chicken, instead of serving it straight up (which you can still do, if you prefer). Make this dish 1–2 days ahead of time, as the chicken needs some time to get drunk.

DRUNKEN CHICKEN

Serves 4

MARINADE

1¼ tablespoons caster (superfine) sugar
2½ tablespoons white soy sauce
200 ml (7 fl oz) Shaoxing wine
4 cm (1½ inch) piece ginger, roughly sliced
1 spring onion (scallion), cut into 5 cm (2 inch) batons

Add all the ingredients and 150 ml (5 fl oz) water to a saucepan over a high heat and bring to the boil. Remove from the heat and leave to cool.

THE REST

2 x 500 g (1 lb 2 oz) spatchcocks (poussin), butterflied
few drops sesame oil
1 small handful of baby coriander (cilantro) leaves, to serve
2 cm (¾ inch) piece young ginger, cut into very thin matchsticks, to serve
sea salt flakes, to serve

Using a sharp knife, remove all bones from the spatchcocks, making sure you don't pierce or tear the skin of the birds. Once all bones are removed, carefully separate the skin from the meat, keeping the skin in one piece. Cut the meat into two breast pieces and two thigh pieces per bird.

Working 1 bird at a time, spread the skin on a chopping board; it should look slightly rectangular. Put two thigh pieces side by side in the middle of the skin, topped with the two breast pieces, laying them side by side and almost interlocking, so there are no gaps.

Carefully fold the sides of the skin in and then roll the whole piece up into a neat cigar shape, just like rolling a rice paper roll.

Spread two large pieces of plastic wrap on the bench, one on top of the other. Put the spatchcock to one end and roll the bundle up tightly to make a neat cigar shape. Tie a knot at each end with kitchen string – it should look like a tight cylinder.

Because you're going to poach the parcel, it's really important to make sure you get this step right. Repeat with the second spatchcock.

Lower the spatchcock parcels into a saucepan of water simmering at 64°C (147°F) and poach for 1 hour. Transfer to a bowl of iced water to cool. Once that's done, remove the parcels from the water and cut off about 5 mm (¼ inch) from the end of each. Unwrap the ballotines from the plastic wrap and immerse in the marinating liquid. Refrigerate for 1–2 days.

Slice the ballotines into 1 cm (½ inch) rounds and arrange them on a plate with a few tablespoons of the marinade, a few drops of sesame oil, some baby coriander, the ginger and a sprinkling of sea salt flakes.

HONG HACKS
To poach, we use an immersion circulator in the kitchen, but it is easily done on the stove over a low heat with a clip-on meat thermometer.

If you don't feel up to doing the ballotine of chicken yourself, ask your butcher to debone, roll and truss the chicken for you. Alternatively, you can use deboned pieces of chicken (skin on) and follow the poaching and marinating process as normal. Either way, drunken chicken is always served cold, sliced and dressed.

DEBONING AND ROLLING CHICKEN

Deboning and rolling chicken is a slightly more advanced technique, but a pretty cool one to master. Your knife must be super sharp and if you want a head start, get your butcher to butterfly your birds. Your goal is not to pierce the skin, so go slow and take care.

Using a sharp knife, remove all bones from the spatchcocks, making sure you don't pierce or tear the skin of the birds. Once all bones are removed, carefully separate the skin from the meat, keeping the skin in one piece. Cut the meat into two breast pieces and two thigh pieces.

Spread the skin on a chopping board; it should look slightly rectangular. Put the two thigh pieces side by side in the middle of the skin, topped with the two breast pieces, laying them side by side and almost interlocking, so there are no gaps.

Carefully fold the sides of the skin in and then roll the whole piece up into a neat cigar shape, just like rolling a rice paper roll.

Spread two large pieces of plastic wrap on the bench, one on top of the other. Put the chicken to one end and roll the bundle up tightly to make a neat cigar shape. Tie a knot at each end with kitchen string – it should look like a tight cylinder.

This is a variation on a classic Chinese dish that incorporates century egg, silken tofu and pork floss. When we were creating this dish, we needed something to stand up to the strong flavour of the preserved egg and dressing. My sous chef at the time, Nigel Stanley, suggested we use smoked eel, which works really well with those flavours and ups the umami factor.

SILKEN TOFU, SMOKED EEL and CENTURY EGG

Serves 3

VINAIGRETTE

2 teaspoons chilli oil
1 tablespoon sesame oil
1½ tablespoons grapeseed oil
2½ tablespoons rice wine vinegar
80 ml (2½ fl oz/⅓ cup) sugar syrup (Essentials, page 240)
100 ml (3½ fl oz) soy sauce
1 garlic clove, microplaned into fine slivers
2 cm (¾ inch) piece ginger, microplaned into fine slivers

Whisk all the ingredients in a bowl together with 1¾ tablespoons water. Set aside.

THE REST

150 g (5½ oz) shimeji mushrooms, trimmed
750 ml (26 fl oz/3 cups) pickling liquor (Essentials, page 241)
2 preserved century eggs
250 g (9 oz) round silken tofu, cut into 1 cm (½ inch) slices
150 g (5½ oz) piece of smoked eel fillet (skinned and deboned), cut into 9 even pieces
2 spring onions (scallions), thinly sliced
fried shallots (Essentials, page 242), to serve

Put the mushrooms in a container and cover with the pickling liquid. Leave to marinate for at least 2 hours.

Fill a small saucepan with cold water and heat over a high heat. Add the century eggs to the saucepan and bring to the boil, then reduce to a simmer for 6 minutes. Drain the eggs and run them under cold water until completely cool. Cut each egg into 6 pieces lengthways (like little wedges).

TO SERVE

Divide 9 slices of tofu among three plates and top each slice with a piece of smoked eel. Whisk the vinaigrette and spoon about two tablespoons over each plate. Top with a few pickled mushrooms, some wedges of century egg, spring onions and fried shallots.

HONG HACKS

Shimeji mushrooms are available at farmers' markets and Asian grocery stores. You can reserve the discarded bits of the mushrooms to make a stock.

Century eggs (also called thousand-year eggs or preserved eggs) are a Chinese delicacy. They are available from Asian grocery stores.

I love pig's ears and I wanted to put them on the menu somehow. What I decided to do was a version of Peking beef, but using pig's ears: you know, that dish of crispy battered matchsticks of beef, coated in thick, sweet sauce. I like this dish because you get that crispy outer layer of pork skin and a soft, gelatinous texture inside. The sweet and sour sauce also helps to balance the richness of the ears.

PEKING-STYLE PIG'S EARS

Serves 4–6 as part of a banquet

PIG'S EARS
10 pig's ears
3 litres (105 fl oz/12 cups) Chinese masterstock (Essentials, page 234)
potato starch, for dusting

Using a kitchen blowtorch (or barbecue gas lighter), burn off any excess hairs that are still attached to the ears. Add the masterstock to a large saucepan, bring to the boil then add the ears. Cover the surface of the liquid with a sheet of baking paper. Braise the ears at a slow simmer for about 3 hours when they should be soft, sticky and gelatinous. Carefully remove them from the masterstock with a slotted spoon and spread on a tray. Once they have cooled down, put the tray in the fridge for the ears to cool completely and solidify.

THE SAUCE
150 ml (5 fl oz) sweet and sour sauce (recipe, page 181)
150 ml (5 fl oz) fish fragrant sauce (recipe, page 186)

Whisk the sweet and sour sauce with the fish fragrant sauce in a bowl. Set aside.

CARROTS
2 carrots
vegetable oil, for deep-frying

Peel and cut the carrots into 3 pieces. Using a mandolin or a vegetable peeler, thinly slice the carrot pieces lengthways to form fine ribbons. Cut the ribbons into very thin matchsticks.

Fill a wok or deep-fryer one-third full with oil and heat to 160°C (315°F) or until a cube of bread dropped into the oil turns golden in 30–35 seconds. Fry the carrot matchsticks for about 2 minutes, until bright yellow and crisp. Drain on paper towels, cover and keep warm.

TO SERVE
2 spring onions (scallions), thinly sliced into rounds, to garnish

Increase the temperature of the deep-fryer oil to 180°C (350°F) or until a cube of bread dropped into the oil turns golden in 15 seconds. Cut the pig's ears into strips about 1 cm (½ inch) wide. Dust the strips in potato starch and fry them in batches for about 5 minutes, or until crisp. Drain on paper towels.

Put the ears in a large bowl and spoon the sauce in. Stir well to ensure everything is evenly coated, then transfer to a serving platter. Garnish with the crispy carrots and spring onions and serve with steamed rice.

Two iconic Australian suburban Chinese dishes have to be honey chicken and lemon chicken. In this recipe, I combine both and use chicken wings… because I love them. It's a terribly simple dish and super popular at Mr Wong.

HONEY LEMON CHICKEN WINGS

Serves 4 as a snack

CHICKEN WINGS
100 ml (3½ fl oz) Shaoxing wine
1½ tablespoons sesame oil
2 tablespoons salt
2 tablespoons caster (superfine) sugar
30 g (1 oz) chicken stock (bouillon) powder
10 g (¼ oz) Chinese five-spice
20 chicken wings, wing tips cut off, separated into wings and drumettes

To make a marinade, put all the ingredients except the chicken wings in a large bowl and mix thoroughly. Add the wings and massage the marinade into them with your hands. Cover with plastic wrap and refrigerate overnight.

HONEY LEMON SAUCE
500 g (1 lb 2 oz) honey
150 ml (5 fl oz) freshly squeezed lemon juice
2 tablespoons potato starch, mixed with a little water to make a slurry
zest of 2 lemons

Put the honey and lemon juice in a saucepan over a high heat and bring to the boil. Start adding the slurry slowly in a steady stream, whisking constantly as you go. Stop when you reach the consistency of golden syrup (you may not need all of the slurry).

Remove the sauce from the heat and add the lemon zest. When cool, transfer to an airtight container and refrigerate until it's required. Bring the sauce to room temperature before you coat the wings.

THE REST
vegetable oil, for deep-frying
sesame seeds, to garnish

Fill a large heavy-based saucepan or deep-fryer to one-third full with oil and heat to 180°C (350°F) or until a cube of bread dropped into the oil turns golden in 15 seconds. Fry the wings in batches to avoid overcrowding and to ensure they cook evenly. Fry for about 7 minutes, until golden. Remove the wings with a wire scoop and put in a bowl. When they are all done, add enough honey lemon sauce to coat the wings evenly. Toss well. Serve on a large plate, garnished with sesame seeds.

HONG HACK
This recipe is awesome for groups of people – just flex up the quantities and make sure you cook the wings in batches so they're crisp and golden.

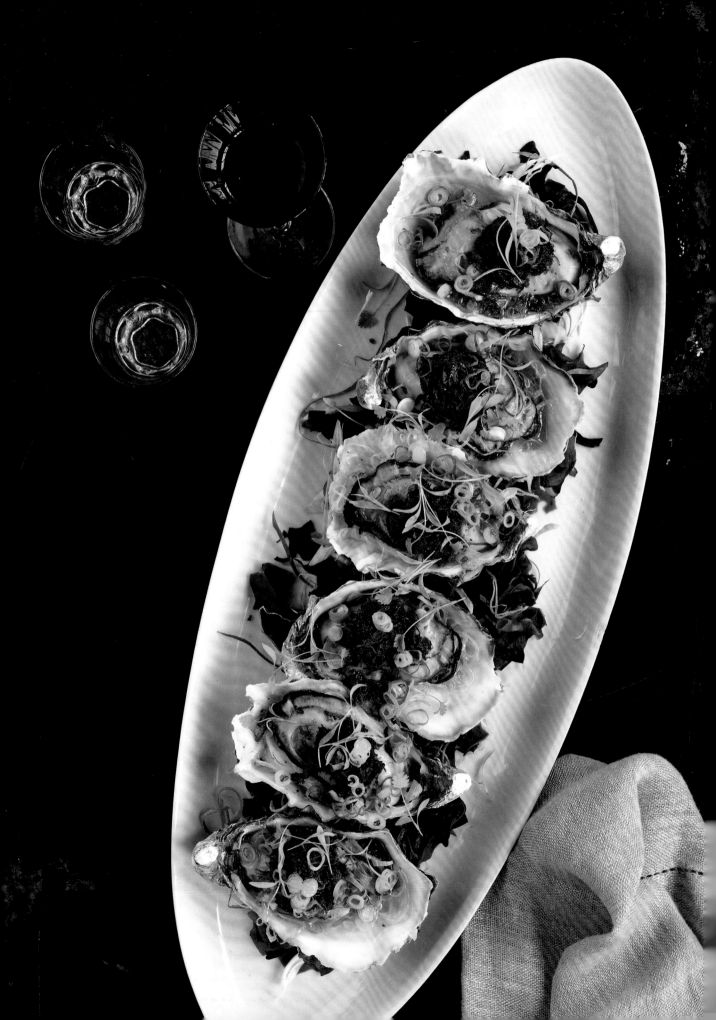

I almost always order this dish when I go to a Chinese restaurant. I like to use really huge Pacific oysters in it because that's what they are best for (anyone who eats those things raw is doing it wrong). When cooked, the texture of these giant oysters is transformed into something fantastic.

STEAMED PACIFIC OYSTERS
with XO, VERMICELLI, GINGER and SHALLOTS

Serves 6 as an entrée

100 g (3½ oz) fine dried rice vermicelli
18 large Pacific oysters
6 cm (2½ inch) piece ginger, cut into thin matchsticks
150 ml (5 fl oz) white soy dressing (Essentials, page 238)
150 ml (5 fl oz) ginger oil (Essentials, page 238)
2¼ tablespoons XO sauce (Essentials, page 239)
3 spring onions (scallions), thinly sliced, to garnish
1 bunch baby coriander (cilantro), leaves only, to garnish

Put the vermicelli in a bowl and cover with boiling water. Leave for 1 minute, drain, then refresh under cold running water. Cut the vermicelli with scissors to make them easier to manage.

Gently remove each oyster from its shell. Put a small bed of vermicelli noodles on the bottom of each shell and replace the oyster. Top this with a few ginger matchsticks. Steam the oysters in batches in a bamboo steamer over a saucepan of boiling water for about 2 minutes.

While the oysters are steaming, warm the white soy dressing in a small saucepan. In another small saucepan, heat the ginger oil to smoking point.

TO SERVE

Once the oysters are cooked, top each one with ½ teaspoon XO sauce and some sliced spring onion. Spoon the warmed white soy dressing all over each oyster. Carefully spoon 1 teaspoon of smoking hot ginger oil over each oyster, and be aware the oil will spit. Garnish with coriander leaves and dig in.

HONG HACKS
If you don't have ginger oil on hand and can't be bothered to make it, use peanut oil instead.

Didn't make XO sauce? Buy it, I won't tell.

Wonton soup is one of my most favourite things to eat in the world. Ever. Sorry Australia, but not a lot of places do a proper job of this dish. Some cheat by using chicken powder to amp up broths, unlike in Hong Kong where almost everyone makes their own superior stock, using Chinese ham, dried shrimp, dried scallops and other richly flavoured ingredients. It's worth the trouble as the results are like night and day.

KING PRAWN WONTONS
in SUPREME BROTH

Serves 4

THE PRAWNS
12 medium king prawns (shrimp), peeled and deveined
1 teaspoon salt
1 teaspoon caster (superfine) sugar
2 teaspoons sesame oil
1 teaspoon potato starch
12 gow gee wrappers

THE SUPREME BROTH
1 litre (35 fl oz/4 cups) supreme stock (Essentials, page 234)
1¼ tablespoons salt
2 tablespoons caster (superfine) sugar
2 tablespoons kombu extract

THE REST
⅓ bunch white garlic chives, snipped into 2 cm (¾ inch) lengths
12 coriander (cilantro) leaves
sesame oil, for serving
about 1 teaspoon dried shrimp roe, to garnish

Put the prawns in a bowl with the salt, sugar, sesame oil and potato starch. Mix well then cover and set aside to marinate for 20 minutes.

Assemble the wontons by first placing a prawn in the middle of each gow gee wrapper. Moisten the edges of the wrappers with a little water. Working one at a time, fold the wrapper ends up to meet each other and press them together to seal, making sure you squeeze out any air pockets in the wonton as you go.

For the supreme broth, bring the supreme stock to the boil in a medium saucepan and add the salt, sugar and kombu extract. Taste, and add more salt if necessary.

Bring a large deep saucepan of water to the boil. Drop the wontons in carefully and cook for about 3 minutes. Scoop the wontons out with a slotted spoon and divide among four bowls. Bring the broth back to the boil and pour over the wontons. Garnish with garlic chives, coriander leaves, a few drops of sesame oil and about one-quarter of a teaspoon of dried shrimp roe on each. Serve immediately.

My favourite way to prepare any seafood is to steam it with ginger and shallots. It's one of the most iconic flavour profiles to come out of Cantonese cuisine. And for good reason: it's light, balanced and lets the seafood show its true character. I decided to use white soy because it's a lot sweeter, less salty and looks prettier on the plate. White soy is traditionally Japanese, so like a lot of dishes, this one's not trying to be traditional. This dressing can be used for whole fish, prawns and scallops or any seafood you want to serve steamed. It's also great with white-cut chicken, too.

STEAMED LOBSTER with WHITE SOY, GINGER and SHALLOTS

Serves 4

1 live rock lobster, about 1.4 kg (3 lb 2 oz)
3 cm (1¼ inch) piece ginger, cut into
thin matchsticks
3 spring onions (scallions), thinly sliced
200 ml (7 fl oz) white soy dressing (Essentials,
page 238)
100 ml (3½ fl oz) ginger oil (Essentials, page 238)
1 big handful of coriander (cilantro) leaves,
to garnish

To kill the lobster, put it in the freezer for about 1 hour to send it to sleep. Remove it from the freezer and work quickly. Grab yourself a chopping board and put the lobster upside down on it. Pierce the shell between the legs with a sharp knife, forcing the knife down to the board. This will leave a large incision for you to cut the whole lobster in half lengthways. Remove and discard the digestive tract, lungs and stomach sac then cut each side in half, through the shell.

Put the lobster pieces on a large plate inside a large bamboo steamer, making sure they are not on top of each other. Top the lobster with the ginger, cover with a tight-fitting lid and place the steamer over a saucepan of boiling water to steam for 4–5 minutes or until it is cooked. Remove the plate from the steamer and scatter most of the spring onions over the lobster. If you transfer the lobster to another plate, be sure not to lose the juice from the lobster, as it forms part of the sauce. Cover and keep warm.

TO SERVE

In a small saucepan, bring the white soy dressing to a simmer and pour it over the lobster. Heat another small saucepan over a high heat until it reaches smoking point, then add the ginger oil and swirl it around for a few seconds. Using a clean, dry spoon, carefully pour 2–3 teaspoons of the boiling oil over each portion of lobster. The oil will spit a little, so be very careful! Garnish with coriander leaves and the rest of the spring onions and serve at once.

The Australian crayfish is one of the best-eating seafood creatures in the world, especially those out of Tasmania and South Australia, where the water is colder. The flavour and texture is pure luxury. This is a classic Chinese dish in a lot of ways – the efu noodles have a spongy, almost chewy texture that's great for soaking up the sauce with all those flavours. This is an extravagant dish for impressing people, which is why it's usually a fixture on any banquet table during Chinese New Year celebrations, or when the in-laws come to visit.

BRAISED EFU NOODLES
with LOBSTER

Serves 4–6

1 live lobster, about 1 kg (2 lb 4 oz)
salt and caster (superfine) sugar, for seasoning
2 cm (¾ inch) piece of ginger, cut into
thin matchsticks
100 g (3½ oz) dried efu noodles
vegetable oil, for frying
½ teaspoon finely chopped garlic
200 ml (7 fl oz) supreme stock (Essentials, page 234)
1½ tablespoons oyster sauce
6 shiitake mushrooms, stalks removed, thinly sliced
½ bunch white garlic chives, cut into 5 cm
(2 inch) lengths
1½ tablespoons Shaoxing wine
1 teaspoon sesame oil
1 teaspoon dried shrimp roe

To kill the lobster, put it in the freezer for about 1 hour to send it to sleep. Remove the lobster from the freezer and quickly put it upside down on a chopping board. Using a large sharp knife, pierce the shell between the lobster's legs, forcing the knife down to the board. This will leave a large incision for you to then cut the whole lobster in half lengthways. Leave the head on (discard the legs) and cut each half into 2 pieces. Remove and discard the digestive tract, lungs and stomach sac from the tail and cut it into 3 cm (1¼ inch) pieces, through the shell.

Arrange the pieces on a large plate, making sure they're not on top of each other. Season the lobster with a little salt and sugar and top with the ginger. Place the plate in a large bamboo steamer over a saucepan of simmering water to steam for about 4–5 minutes, or until the lobster is just cooked through. Set aside in a warm place.

Bring a large saucepan of water to the boil and blanch the noodles for 30 seconds until tender. Drain, refresh with cold water to stop the cooking process and set aside.

Heat a wok or large frying pan over a medium heat and add a little oil. Add the garlic and fry for about 20 seconds, or until fragrant. Stir in the supreme stock, oyster sauce and 1 teaspoon each of salt and sugar. Add the noodles and shiitake mushrooms. Braise for about 1 minute, before adding the lobster and garlic chives. Turn off the heat and stir in the Shaoxing wine and sesame oil. Transfer to a serving plate and sprinkle the shrimp roe on top. Serve immediately.

BREAKING DOWN LOBSTER

It's ok, you can do this! If you're a bit nervous about killing live seafood, the most important tip is to put the little guy in the freezer for just long enough for it to go to sleep. It takes away the 'mobility' factor, making the whole thing a lot easier to do.

Pierce the shell between the legs with a sharp knife,

Force the knife down to the board.

This will leave a large incision for you to cut the whole lobster in half lengthways.

Remove and discard the digestive tract, lungs and stomach sac then cut each side in half, through the shell.

Real Singaporeans know it's all about black pepper crab, not chilli crab! This is not a traditional recipe, but it's ridiculously tasty.

BLACK PEPPER CRAB

Serves 4 as an entrée or 2 as a main course

1 live mud crab
80 g (2¾ oz) unsalted butter
2 tablespoons finely chopped garlic
4 cm (1½ inch) piece ginger, finely chopped
60 g (2¼ oz) ground black pepper
200 ml (7 fl oz) chicken stock (Essentials, page 236)
3 tablespoons oyster sauce
1½ tablespoons caster (superfine) sugar
1½ tablespoons kombu extract (optional)
1 tablespoon salt
3 spring onions (scallions), 2 cut into 3 cm (1¼ inch) lengths, 1 thinly sliced, green part only, to garnish
vegetable oil, for deep-frying
potato starch, for dusting
2½ tablespoons Shaoxing wine
1 tablespoon sesame oil
20 coriander (cilantro) leaves

Put the mud crab in the freezer for 1 hour to send it to sleep. Once asleep, take it from the freezer and work quickly. Turn the crab upside down and make an incision with a sharp, heavy knife into the middle of the body, driving the knife down between the eyes. You can now pull the body out of the shell. Discard the tail, lungs and stomach sac. Wash the crab thoroughly under cold water to remove any mud, and scrub the shells with a clean sponge. Separate the claws and knuckles, and cut the body into 4–6 pieces. Using the back of a heavy knife, carefully crack the claws and knuckles. This makes it much easier to hoe into later.

Heat a wok over a medium–high heat, add the butter and bring it to bubbling point. Just as the butter starts to foam, add the garlic and ginger and cook, stirring continuously, for about 2 minutes until fragrant. Add the pepper and cook for 1 minute, then add the chicken stock, oyster sauce, sugar,

kombu extract and salt. Bring to the boil and simmer until the sauce has reduced by one-third. Add the 3 cm (1¼ inch) lengths of spring onions and cook for 30 seconds before turning the heat off.

Fill a large heavy-based saucepan or deep-fryer one-third full with oil and heat to 180°C (350°F) or until a cube of bread dropped into the oil turns golden in 15 seconds. Dust the crabmeat pieces in potato starch and set aside. Gently lower the claws and knuckles into the hot oil. Be careful as the oil may spit. Fry for 2 minutes and then add the dusted meat pieces. Fry for another 2 minutes, then drain on paper towels.

TO SERVE

Put the wok with the sauce back on the heat, and add the crab pieces. Wok-toss until all pieces are liberally coated. Add the Shaoxing wine and sesame oil, remove from the heat and serve immediately topped with coriander leaves and the thinly sliced spring onions. You can add the shell too, if you like.

I spent about six months trying to nail the perfect salt and pepper squid. In my view, it is Australia's national dish! Think about it – it's not that popular around the rest of the world, but you can find it at any pub, café and restaurant around the country. Different cuisines all have a version and it's almost always the most popular dish on the menu. I gauge a Chinese restaurant based on how well they do their salt and pepper squid. If it's shit, they're probably not very good at anything else. The crispiness of the batter, the softness of the squid – it's a winning combination.

SALT and PEPPER SQUID

Serves 6

2 large whole squid, about 800 g (1 lb 12 oz) each

BATTER
100 g (3½ oz/⅔ cup) glutinous rice flour
100 g (3½ oz/⅔ cup) rice flour
100 g (3½ oz/⅔ cup) tapioca starch
350 ml (12 fl oz) soda water

THE REST
300 g (10½ oz) potato starch, for dusting
vegetable oil, for deep-frying
3 tablespoons finely chopped garlic
5 bird's eye chillies, thinly sliced into rounds
spicy salt (Essentials, page 243)
2 spring onions (scallions), thinly sliced, to garnish
1 small handful of baby coriander (cilantro) leaves, to garnish
lemon cheeks, to garnish

Clean the squid by removing the head and cutting beneath the eyes. Discard the eyes and cut the tentacles into segments. Reserve these. Cut open the main part of the body, discard the guts and wings, pull off the outer skin and reserve the tube only. With a sharp knife, score the underside and then cut it into rectangular pieces about 2 x 5 cm (¾ x 2 inches). At the end, you should be left with the tentacles and scored tube pieces.

Make the batter by combining the glutinous rice flour, rice flour and tapioca starch in a bowl. Add the soda water and whisk until well combined. The batter should not be too thick but have an almost runny texture. Put the potato starch in another bowl.

Dip a few squid pieces in the batter, then into the bowl of potato starch, turning the pieces until they feel dry. Repeat the process with the rest of

the squid and store in a dry container. They can be kept in the fridge like this, uncovered, for up to 30 minutes.

Fill a small frying pan with 3 cm (1¼ inches) of oil, heat over a medium–high heat and shallow-fry the garlic and chilli until golden brown. Drain on paper towels.

Fill a large wok or deep-fryer to one-third full with oil and heat to 200°C (400°F) or until a cube of bread dropped into the oil turns golden in 15 seconds. Carefully drop in the squid in batches, making sure the pieces don't stick together, and fry for 2 minutes or so or until crisp. Don't expect the batter to turn golden, because the starches we've used don't take on a lot of colour, especially if you are using new oil. Remove the squid with a wire scoop and drain on paper towels to absorb excess oil. Sprinkle liberally with spicy salt.

Assemble the squid on a plate and top with the spring onions, fried garlic and chilli. Garnish with coriander leaves and lemon cheeks. Serve immediately.

HONG HACK
If you can't handle breaking down whole squid yourself, buy squid tubes that are already cleaned. Simply cut them into pieces as outlined in the recipe.

Everyone knows about mapo tofu. It's one of the most famous dishes to come out of the Sichuan province. My other favourite cuisine is Japanese and I'm completely obsessed with chawanmushi. It's like the best savoury crème brûlée. When I created this dish, I wanted to make a custard, rather than just serving it with tofu. The soy milk gives it that tofu element, and I love scooping into this dish – a bit of spicy, slightly numbing pork mince on the top and then the silky savoury custard at the bottom. It's an awesome contrast and partnership at the same time. This dish will serve two as a main meal with rice, or several people as a starter if you steam the custard in smaller, individually portioned ramekins.

MAPO TOFU

Serves 2

MARINATED PORK
1 tablespoon soy sauce
1 tablespoon sesame oil
1 teaspoon sugar
1 teaspoon salt
300 g (10½ oz) minced (ground) pork

Combine the soy sauce, sesame oil, sugar and salt in a bowl. Add the minced pork and work it through the marinade using clean hands. Set aside.

SOY MILK CUSTARD
400 ml (14½ fl oz) unsweetened soy milk
175 g (6 oz) whole eggs (about 4 medium eggs), lightly beaten
3 tablespoons white soy sauce

Firstly, find a suitable bowl or bowls that will fit inside your steamer basket when the lid is on. Next, whisk the soy milk, eggs and white soy sauce in a bowl to combine, then divide the mixture evenly between the bowls. Cover each bowl with plastic wrap, tight enough so the plastic won't sag during cooking and touch the surface of the custard.

Put the bowls in the steamer basket with a tight-fitting lid, then place over a saucepan of simmering water for 15–18 minutes, or until the custard is set but still a little soft to the touch. You can test if the custard is ready by removing the plastic and lightly touching the surface with your finger. If there's a bit of bounce, but it feels firm, then it's done. Set aside, and keep warm.

THE REST
vegetable oil, for frying
1 tablespoon chopped ginger
1 tablespoon chopped garlic
1 tablespoon chopped red chilli
1 tablespoon ground Sichuan pepper, plus extra, to serve
2 tablespoons caster (superfine) sugar
2 tablespoons chilli bean paste
2 tablespoons soy sauce
2 tablespoons oyster sauce
100 ml (3½ fl oz) chicken stock (Essentials, page 236)
splash of Shaoxing wine
1 tablespoon chilli oil
3 spring onions (scallions), thinly sliced, and 1 small handful of finely chopped coriander (cilantro) stalks
coriander (cilantro), leaves only, to garnish

Heat a wok over a high heat and add a little vegetable oil. Fry the pork mince, breaking it up with a wooden spoon as you stir-fry continuously. Once the pork is three-quarters cooked, add the ginger, garlic, chilli and Sichuan pepper. Stir-fry for about 15 seconds, then add the sugar, chilli bean paste, soy and oyster sauces and cook for a further 15 seconds.

Add the chicken stock and cook until the liquid has reduced to your desired consistency. You'll know when it's done as the sauce should coat the meat but still be 'saucy'. Remove the wok from the heat and add the Shaoxing wine and chilli oil.

Gently ladle the pork over the cooked custards. Top with a little extra ground Sichuan pepper and garnish with the spring onions and coriander leaves. Serve with steamed rice.

This is my ode to Australians and how much we love lamb chops. Also, I love that you can pretty much salt and pepper anything and we'll eat it. Mr Wong is all about mixing traditional Chinese dishes with ones that put a twist on culture... and this is one of them.

SALT and PEPPER LAMB CUTLETS

Serves 4

4 lamb cutlets

MARINADE
150 g (5½ oz) white fermented tofu
1½ tablespoons finely grated garlic
2 tablespoons Knorr Liquid Seasoning
3¾ tablespoons Shaoxing wine

Using a mallet or rolling pin, lightly bash the lamb cutlets until they are slightly flattened out.

Whisk all the marinade ingredients together in a large bowl until the tofu is smooth. Add the cutlets and, wearing a pair of food prep gloves (unless you like stinky hands), massage the marinade into the meat. Cover the bowl and refrigerate overnight.

FENNEL AND CUMIN SALT
100 g (3½ oz) cumin seeds
50 g (1¾ oz) fennel seeds
100 g (3½ oz/¾ cup) sea salt
2½ tablespoons caster (superfine) sugar

Roast the cumin and fennel seeds in a dry frying pan or wok over a medium heat until they colour slightly and become fragrant. Transfer them to a spice grinder and add the salt and sugar. Grind to a fine powder then store in an airtight container.

1 serve batter mix (Salt and pepper squid recipe, page 165)

THE REST
200 g (7 oz) water chestnut flour
vegetable oil, for frying
1½ tablespoons finely chopped garlic
2 bird's eye chillies, thinly sliced into rounds
coriander (cilantro) leaves, to garnish
1 spring onion (scallion), thinly sliced
lemon wedges, to serve

Remove the lamb from the fridge about 30 minutes before you're ready to cook. Mix the batter ingredients. Put the water chestnut flour in a bowl. Dip the cutlets in the batter and then press them into the water chestnut flour, making sure that the whole cutlet is covered and feels dry.

Add about 3 cm (1¼ inches) of oil to a small frying pan over a medium heat and shallow-fry the garlic and chilli until the garlic turns golden brown. Drain on paper towels.

Fill a wok or deep-fryer to one-third full with oil and heat to 180°C (350°F) or until a cube of bread dropped into the oil turns golden in 15 seconds. Deep-fry the cutlets, two at a time, for about 4 minutes, or until golden. Drain on paper towels and leave to rest for about 2 minutes. Coat both sides liberally with the fennel and cumin salt. Put on a serving plate and top with the fried garlic and chilli then garnish with the coriander leaves and spring onions and serve with lemon wedges.

ROAST
DUCK

When I started planning for Mr Wong, I thought about how hard it was going to be to do a proper Chinese roast duck. It's a speciality that takes people a lifetime to master, and there was no way we'd have a Chinese restaurant without roast duck. Jow and I spent about three months at Ms G's experimenting every which way with duck: hanging them in the cool room to dry out the skin, different brining recipes and lacquer combinations. We watched YouTube, read books, Jow even staged at some Chinese BBQ restaurants in Chinatown to try to learn from the masters. Here's the thing though: they're really secretive. There was always a stage they did themselves and didn't allow him to see. In the end, we used a combination of our BBQ chef Jack's knowledge and our own ideas and research until we were confident we had nailed it. We've basically sold out of duck every day since we opened, so we must have done something right.

This recipe is a little fiddly, but it's worth trying if you like to eat roast duck. You can of course, go to Chinatown and buy them (and they can be awesome), but sometimes it's more satisfying to make yourself. The process is a bit lengthy – allow 24 hours for brining and another 24 hours to hang and dry out the duck before cooking. This process will ensure the duck is juicy, but the skin is super crisp. Ideally, you'll need to remove the racks in your oven so you can roast the duck, hanging vertically.

ROAST DUCK

Serves 16 as an entrée or 8 as a main course

DAY 1

BRINE
500 g (1 lb 2 oz) salt
150 g (5½ oz/⅔ cup) caster (superfine) sugar
400 ml (14 fl oz) kombu extract
10 quills of cassia bark
20 star anise
3 tablespoons Sichuan peppercorns
10 cm (4 inch) piece of ginger, sliced
1 bunch spring onions (scallions), green part only
500 ml (17 fl oz/2 cups) Chinese rose wine

2 x 1.8 kg (4 lb) whole fresh ducks
900 ml (31 fl oz) maltose liquor (recipe, page 177)

For the brine, fill a large stockpot with 8 litres (280 fl oz/32 cups) water, then add all the brining ingredients and whisk to combine. Keep on whisking until the salt and sugar have completely dissolved.

Trim the wing tips off the ducks and discard. Put the ducks in the brine and cover with a weighted plate to make sure they remain fully submerged for 24 hours.

DAYS 2–3

Fill a large wok or saucepan with water and bring to the boil. Attach a butcher's hook underneath each of the duck's wings, where they meet the body. Using the hooks to hold onto the duck, dip one into the boiling water to blanch it. Then, holding the duck over the water, use a large ladle to scoop boiling water all over the skin. Do this a few times – you will notice that the skin will start to tighten. (Tightening the skin allows it to dry out properly, which will give you a super-crisp texture at the end.) Repeat with the second duck.

As soon as you're done blanching the ducks, dip them in the maltose liquor, using the same process as blanching (ladling over the maltose liquor to cover all areas of the skin). Now hang the ducks in a warm dry place (off a cupboard over a sink works well) and leave for about 5 hours to make sure the skin dries out. Transfer the ducks to a tray and leave in the fridge uncovered for 24 hours.

Remove the ducks from the fridge a few hours before you want to roast them. Having them at room temperature makes the ducks easiers to cook and ensures the skin is dry and will crisp up.

Before you turn the oven on, reconfigure it so the ducks can hang vertically. You might want to put a tray with water in it on the bottom so the fat can drip down without messing up your oven. Preheat the oven to 230°C (450°F/Gas 8).

Hang the ducks in the oven over the tray and roast for 50–60 minutes. Halfway through cooking, check how they're going and rotate the ducks as they will brown unevenly if you don't turn them around.

Take the ducks from the oven as soon as they are ready and carve them. The longer you leave them, the less crisp the skin becomes.

In most Chinese restaurants roast duck is served in one of two ways. Firstly, the skin and a little bit of meat might be served Peking-style on pancakes (which you can buy ready-made at most Asian grocery stores), along with a baton each of spring onion and cucumber, and a little bit of hoisin sauce. The rest of the meat is then removed from the bone, shredded and tossed with noodles or fried rice. Alternatively, the duck is carved as you would with any roast bird. I like to keep the juices from carving, mix them with a little bit of white soy dressing and pour it back over the carved pieces. It's also delicious served with plum sauce.

HONG HACK
We have duck ovens built for the express purpose of roasting ducks at Mr Wong. Logistically, this recipe becomes a whole lot more difficult at home where ovens might be too small or impossible to configure to hang the ducks vertically. If you can't reconfigure the oven, lay them on a lightly greased wire rack inside a baking tray and turn regularly to ensure the skin is evenly crisped on all sides.

I love eating small birds. Pigeon (aka squab) has to be one of my favourite birds to eat. It's so expensive, but worth it. The flavour of the meat is a bit like gamey duck – it's the crab of poultry – and so good that it's worth picking over every last bone and working for the meat. Start this dish a day ahead, as the birds need some time to hang out before cooking.

ROAST PIGEON

Serves 4–6 as part of a banquet

BRINE
110 g (3¾ oz/½ cup) caster (superfine) sugar
110 g (3¾ oz) salt
1 tablespoon Chinese five-spice
15 star anise
2 cinnamon sticks
10 cloves
1 tablespoon fennel seeds
500 g (1 lb 2 oz) ice

For the brine, fill a large saucepan with 500 ml (17 fl oz/2 cups) water, add all the ingredients except for the ice and heat over a high heat. When boiling point is reached, take off the heat and add the ice, which will immediately cool the mixture.

MALTOSE LIQUOR
200 g (7 oz) maltose
700 ml (24 fl oz) Chinese red vinegar
1½ tablespoons sugar

THE REST
4 x 500 g (1 lb 2 oz) pigeons
vegetable oil, for frying
spicy salt (Essentials, page 243), for serving
lemon wedges, for serving

For the maltose liquor, whisk all the ingredients together in a bowl, and keep whisking until the maltose and sugar have completely dissolved.

Trim the wing tips off the pigeons and discard. Put the birds in the brine and cover with a weighted plate to make sure they remain fully submerged for 24 hours.

After about 2 hours take the birds out of the brine and attach a butcher's hook underneath each wing of each bird, as you will need to hang them later.

Bring a deep saucepan of water to the boil. Holding onto the butcher's hooks, carefully blanch the pigeons in the boiling water, lifting them in and out of the water several times to tighten the skin, just like a teabag commercial in the 1990s. Do this for about 15 seconds. After blanching, dip the whole bird in the maltose liquor several times (again, for 15 seconds or so). Hang the birds in a dry and cool room until their skin is very dry. This will take about 24 hours, but if you can't do that, at least hang them for a few hours, but overnight is even better.

Fill a large heavy-based saucepan or deep-fryer to one-third full with oil and heat to 200°C (400°F) or until a cube of bread dropped into the oil turns golden in 5 seconds. Fry each bird for 5–7 minutes, until the skin is golden but the meat is still a little pink. If you aren't sure whether the pigeon is done, use a meat thermometer to check the internal temperature, which should be around 65°C (150°F).

Transfer the birds to a wire rack sitting in a roasting tin and rest them for about 5 minutes before carving. Chop each pigeon into six pieces, straight through the bones, and serve immediately with the spiced salt and lemon wedges.

HONG HACKS
If you can't find maltose, use the same amount of honey instead. Maltose is available from gourmet food stores.

Even if you're cooking fewer birds, you still need the same amount of brine and maltose/honey liquor.

This famous spicy chicken dish originated in Sichuan and gained cult status in America. I will always remember the *Seinfeld* episode where George Costanza is accused of stealing while eating kung pao. His boss thinks he's lying because he's sweating so much but George blames it on the spiciness of the dish. 'George likes his chicken spicy!' One time, an order came through the restaurant, which read '1 kung pao – not spicy' I laughed and thought it was a joke. I mean seriously, 'DO YOU EVEN KUNG PAO?' Order something else!

KUNG PAO CHICKEN

Serves 2

MARINATED CHICKEN
1 tablespoon light soy sauce
1¼ tablespoons Shaoxing wine
1 teaspoon chicken stock (bouillon) powder
1 teaspoon caster (superfine) sugar
3 teaspoons sesame oil
500 g (1 lb 2 oz) chicken thigh fillets, cut into 2 cm (¾ inch) dice

To marinate the chicken, whisk together in a bowl the soy sauce, Shaoxing wine, stock powder, sugar and sesame oil with a good pinch of salt. Add the chicken and stir to coat the pieces well. Cover the bowl with plastic wrap and refrigerate for at least 2 hours.

THE REST
vegetable oil, for frying
1½ teaspoons finely chopped garlic
1 handful of dried red chillies
3 spring onions (scallions), white part only, cut into 3 cm (1¼ inch) lengths
80 g (2¾ oz) roasted peanuts
4 green garlic chives, snipped into 3 cm (1¼ inch) lengths
4 tablespoons soy paste
2 tablespoons Lao Gan Ma chilli oil (with peanuts)
2 teaspoons caster (superfine) sugar
2 teaspoons Chinkiang black vinegar
½ teaspoon ground Sichuan pepper

Heat 2 tablespoons of oil in a wok over a high heat. When it reaches smoking point, fry the chicken in batches until caramelised and cooked through. Remove each batch from the wok and put in a bowl.

Add more oil to the pan and fry the garlic and whole dried chillies until fragrant – the chillies should smell roasted. Add the spring onions, peanuts and garlic chives and stir-fry for 30 seconds. Return the cooked chicken to the wok and add the rest of the ingredients. Stir-fry for 1 minute, or until most of the liquid has evaporated and the sauce starts to caramelise around the meat. The dish should be really fragrant and smell of Sichuan pepper and roasted chilli. Serve immediately as part of a shared meal, with steamed rice and some greens.

Sweet and sour pork was pretty much a staple for Aussie families that grew up between the 1970s and the 1990s. My version is inspired by Longrain's caramelised pork hock dish with Chinese five-spice and chilli vinegar. Start this recipe a day ahead if you're going to go the whole hog and make the terrine.

SWEET and SOUR PORK HOCK

Serves 8 as part of a banquet

DAY 1

PORK HOCKS
8 litres (280 fl oz/32 cups) Chinese masterstock (Essentials, page 234)
6 pork hocks

Add the masterstock to a large stockpot and bring to the boil. Add the pork hocks. Simmer for about 5 hours, or until the hocks are completely soft and gelatinous, and the bones can be removed easily. Transfer the hocks to a tray and leave them until cool enough to handle. Remove all the bones and knuckles, trying not to break up the meat and skin too much.

Line a large roasting tin with baking paper and spread the pork hock meat, fat and skin on it as evenly as possible. Place another piece of baking paper on top, and then sandwich another baking tray on top to compress everything. Use a few heavy jars, or a six-pack of beer to weight the baking tray down. Refrigerate the compressed pork structure overnight.

DAY 2

SWEET AND SOUR SAUCE
2 onions, coarsely chopped
10 garlic cloves
5 cm (2 inch) piece ginger, roughly chopped
1 kg (2 lb 4 oz) caster (superfine) sugar
300 ml (10½ fl oz) Chinese red vinegar
100 ml (3½ fl oz) fish sauce
200 g (7 oz) soy paste
300 ml (10½ fl oz) tomato ketchup

Put the onion, garlic and ginger in the bowl of a food processor and blend until a fine paste forms. Set aside. Fill a wide saucepan with 100 ml (3½ fl oz) water, add the sugar and heat over a medium–high

heat. Resist the urge to stir, just bring to the boil and allow the heat to begin to transform the sugar. It should take about 5–6 minutes to turn a golden caramel colour. During that time, if crystals start to appear you can give the pan a little swirl, or use a wet pastry brush to remove any crystals.

Add the remaining ingredients as well as the reserved paste and simmer everything down until the sauce is thick enough to coat the back of a spoon. Cover and keep warm.

THE REST
vegetable oil, for deep-frying
2 spring onions (scallions), thinly sliced
3 small long red chillies, thinly sliced into rounds
fried shallots (Essentials, page 242), to garnish
coriander (cilantro) leaves, to garnish

Cut the pork terrine into 2 cm (¾ inch) cubes. Fill a large wok or deep-fryer one-third full with oil and heat to 180°C (350°F) or until a cube of bread dropped into the oil turns golden in 15 seconds. Deep-fry about 10 pieces of pork at a time for 3 minutes, or until crisp and golden. Drain each batch on paper towels, then transfer to serving plates and coat liberally with the sweet and sour sauce. Pile the spring onions and chillies on top of each piece, followed by the fried shallots and coriander.

HONG HACK
Pressing the pork into a terrine is great for presentation and impressing the hell out of the in-laws. If you don't need to impress, skip that step and head straight for the deep-fryer. Do not pass go.

Warrigal greens were one of the first Australian vegetables that settlers picked up on. Apparently Captain Cook made convicts eat them in an effort to survive the scourge of scurvy. As they contain oxates, which are toxic when eaten in large quantities (though you'd have to eat a lot), it's advisable to cook them unless you're just using them as a garnish. This dish also celebrates the amazing selection of mushrooms we've managed to cultivate here in Australia, the result being a clean, fresh dish that's a complete vegetarian meal when served with rice, or great as a side dish in a banquet.

WOK-FRIED MUSHROOMS
with WARRIGAL GREENS

Serves 3–4

vegetable oil, for deep-frying
100 g (3½ oz) shimeji mushrooms, base cut off and discarded
100 g (3½ oz) oyster mushrooms
100 g (3½ oz) king brown mushrooms, cut into 5 mm (¼ inch) slices
100 g (3½ oz) shiitake mushrooms, stems removed, caps halved
1½ tablespoons finely chopped garlic
3¾ tablespoons chicken stock (Essentials, page 236)
1½ tablespoons mushroom soy sauce
2 tablespoons soy paste
1 tablespoon salt
1½ tablespoons caster (superfine) sugar
50 g (1¾ oz) fresh wood ear fungus
50 g (1¾ oz) fresh white fungus
50 g (1¾ oz) enoki mushrooms
50 g (1¾ oz) warrigal greens
splash of Shaoxing wine
2 teaspoons sesame oil

Fill a large wok one-third full with oil and heat to 180°C (350°F) or until a cube of bread dropped into the oil turns golden in 15 seconds. Deep-fry the shimeji, oyster, king brown and shiitake mushrooms until golden. Using a slotted spoon, remove the mushrooms from the oil and drain on paper towels. Drain the oil from the wok and return it to the heat. Pour in 2 tablespoons of fresh oil and when hot, add the garlic. Fry for 20 seconds or so, until fragrant.

Return the fried mushrooms to the wok and add the stock, mushroom soy, soy paste, salt and sugar. Braise the mushrooms for 30 seconds. Add the wood ear and white fungus, enoki mushrooms and warrigal greens. Stir-fry until the greens have just wilted, then turn the heat off and add the Shaoxing wine and sesame oil. Serve immediately.

This is another play on a classic Chinese restaurant dish. It's probably not a surprise to anyone that many restaurants use tinned vegetables for this recipe, so by using fresh, good-quality vegetables, this dish becomes an unsung hero on the banquet table. A clay pot is the traditional vessel to serve this dish in.

BRAISED BABY VEGETABLES (LO HUN STYLE)

Serves 2

INGREDIENTS

25 g (1 oz) fine bean-thread vermicelli glass noodles
3 baby carrots, halved lengthways
3 baby turnips, halved
3 x 25 g (1 oz) pieces soft tofu, halved
vegetable oil, for frying
1 teaspoon finely chopped garlic
2 teaspoons finely chopped ginger
3 baby corn, halved lengthways
200 ml (7 fl oz) chicken stock (Essentials, page 236)
2 teaspoons oyster sauce
1 teaspoon salt
1 teaspoon caster (superfine) sugar
1 teaspoon kombu extract
3 zucchini (courgette) flowers, stamen removed, halved lengthways
8 sugarsnap peas, topped and tailed
3 shiitake mushrooms, stems removed, caps halved
6 pieces black fungi
1 tablespoon kuzu (root starch), mixed with
3 tablespoons water to make a slurry
splash of Shaoxing wine
2 teaspoons sesame oil

Start with the noodles. Put them in a bowl and cover with boiling water. After 1 minute, drain, then refresh under cold running water. Drain and set aside.

Blanch the baby carrots and turnips for 1 minute in boiling, lightly salted water. Drain and refresh in iced water to stop the cooking process and keep the tone of the vegetables.

For the tofu, fill a wok or deep-fryer one-third full with oil and heat to 180°C (350°F) or until a cube of bread dropped into the oil turns golden in 15 seconds. Gently lower the tofu into the oil and deep-fry the pieces until crisp and golden. Drain on paper towels and set aside.

Add 2 tablespoons of oil to a wok over a high heat, then add the garlic and ginger and fry quickly, for about 20 seconds, until fragrant, but not coloured. Add the carrots, turnips, tofu and baby corn and stir-fry for about 30 seconds. Add the chicken stock, oyster sauce, salt, sugar and kombu extract and braise the vegetables for 1 minute. Add the zucchini flowers, sugarsnap peas, shiitake and black fungi and braise for another 1 minute. While the sauce is bubbling, carefully pour in the kuzu slurry in a thin stream while stirring continuously. This will thicken the sauce to a glaze-like consistency. Turn the heat off then add the Shaoxing wine and sesame oil.

To assemble, put the noodles in a clay pot and gently ladle the braised vegetables on top. Serve with steamed rice.

HONG HACKS
You can substitute the soft tofu with store-bought deep-fried tofu puffs available from Asian grocery stores.

This dish works better with baby vegetables, but look at what's in season and substitute with whatever baby veg is at its best.

This dish was created by one of my old sous chefs, Victor Liong, after he ate at Dainty Sichuan, Melbourne. Fish fragrant sauce doesn't actually have any fish in it, but the sweet, sour and spicy elements in the sauce are traditionally used to cook Sichuan fish dishes, and it gives this dish its name.

CRISPY EGGPLANT with FISH FRAGRANT SAUCE

Serves 4–6 as part of a banquet

FISH FRAGRANT SAUCE

450 g (1 lb) caster (superfine) sugar
100 g (3½ oz) liquid glucose
100 ml (3½ fl oz) light soy sauce
100 ml (3½ fl oz) Chinese red vinegar
70 g (2½ oz) soy paste
2½ tablespoons Chinkiang black vinegar
2 tablespoons chilli bean paste
2 tablespoons Lao Gan Ma chilli oil (with peanuts)
1 tablespoon very finely chopped ginger
2 tablespoons finely chopped garlic
3 bird's eye chillies, very finely chopped
1 teaspoon salt
2 teaspoons ground Sichuan pepper
½ teaspoon chilli flakes
50 g (1¾ oz/⅓ cup) sesame seeds

Put the sugar and liquid glucose in a large saucepan and add 250 ml (9 fl oz/1 cup) water. Whisk over a medium heat to dissolve the sugar, then increase the heat to high, stirring until the mixture starts to boil. Keep boiling until the temperature reaches 120°C (235°F).

Add the remaining sauce ingredients, stir to combine and leave it to simmer for 1 hour. At the end, you should have a glazy caramel-like consistency, which coats the back of a spoon. This sauce can be stored in a jar in the fridge for up to 2 months.

THE BATTER

15 g (½ oz) xanthan gum
60 g (2¼ oz) rice flour
60 g (2¼ oz) tapioca flour
1 teaspoon salt

Put the xanthan gum and 550 ml (19 fl oz) water into a bowl. Whizz with a hand-held blender until it has a thick, viscous consistency. Blend in the rice and tapioca flours, followed by the salt. The result should be a fairly goopy, but smooth batter.

THE REST

vegetable oil, for deep-frying
6 Japanese eggplants (long thin aubergine), peeled, cut into batons about 5 x 1.5 cm (2 x ⅝ inch)
sprigs from ½ bunch coriander (cilantro), finely chopped
2 small long red chillies, thinly sliced into rounds
2 spring onions (scallions), finely chopped
3 tablespoons fried shallots (Essentials, page 242)
1 small handful of baby coriander leaves and sesame seeds, to garnish

Fill a large wok or deep-fryer one-third full with oil and heat to 180°C (350°F) or until a cube of bread dropped into the oil turns golden in 15 seconds. Dip the pieces of eggplant into the batter then gently lower them into the oil one by one. Fry in batches for about 5 minutes per batch. Don't fiddle around with the eggplant too much in the first 2–3 minutes to allow the batter to firm properly. After about 3 minutes the exterior will harden and you can use a pair of tongs to separate any pieces that have stuck together in the oil. Continue cooking until the 5-minute mark. Drain on paper towels.

TO SERVE

Put the eggplant in a bowl and pour about 100 ml (3½ fl oz) of the fish fragrant sauce on top. Using a large spoon, give everything a stir to make sure each piece of eggplant is evenly coated. Add the coriander sprigs and chillies and mix through. Divide between four to six bowls and top with the spring onions and fried shallots. Sprinkle with baby coriander leaves and sesame seeds.

A traditional Cantonese dish. I love the flavour of dried scallops, they make a brilliant topping for vegetables and add instant umami.

BRAISED SNOW PEA LEAVES
with CONPOY SAUCE

Serves 4

10 large conpoy (dried scallops)
1 tablespoon kuzu (root starch), mixed with
3 tablespoons water to make a slurry
vegetable oil, for frying
1 teaspoon finely chopped garlic
125 g (4½ oz) snow pea (mangetout) leaves, thick and woody stalks removed
3¾ tablespoons supreme stock (Essentials, page 234)
1 teaspoon salt
1 teaspoon caster (superfine) sugar
2½ tablespoons Shaoxing wine

Fill a small bowl with 300 ml (10½ fl oz) water, add the conpoy and cover with foil. Place the bowl in a bamboo steamer over a saucepan of simmering water and steam for 2 hours. Remove the conpoy from the bowl and reserve the liquid as you will need it later. When cool enough to handle, slightly shred the conpoy by squashing them between your fingers.

Bring the steamed conpoy liquid to the boil in a small saucepan. Taste it, it should already be quite seasoned and a little sweet. Adjust the seasoning with a little sugar and/or salt if needed. While the liquid is boiling, thicken it by pouring in the kuzu slurry in a slow stream, stirring constantly. The sauce should thicken up quite a bit. Add the shredded conpoy and remove from the heat.

Heat a wok over a medium–high heat and add a little oil. Fry the garlic until fragrant but not too coloured. Add the snow pea leaves and begin to stir-fry. Add the supreme stock, the salt and sugar and continue stir-frying until the leaves wilt and the stalks become tender.

Transfer the snow pea leaves to a plate. Bring the conpoy sauce back to the boil and, as it starts to simmer, take the pan off the heat and stir in the Shaoxing wine. Spoon the sauce over the top of the leaves and serve immediately.

Every single Cantonese restaurant in the world has mango pudding on the menu. If white people order deep-fried ice cream, then Asians order mango pudding. For Mr Wong, I wanted to give this classic more texture and put my own stamp on it. I added tapioca, those mouth-popping balls that you eat with frozen yoghurt, fresh pomelo and mango, as well as passionfruit granita to accentuate the tropical fruit vibe.

MANGO PUDDING

Serves 4

PASSIONFRUIT GRANITA
100 ml (3½ fl oz) passionfruit pulp (no seeds)
150 ml (5 fl oz) sugar syrup (Essentials, page 240)

Combine both the ingredients in a bowl with 300 ml (10½ fl oz) water. Pour the mixture into an ice-cream tray and put it in the freezer. Every 30 minutes or so, stir the granita with a fork, scraping the ice crystals off the bottom and sides of the tray. Break up any chunks of ice that have formed and return the tray to the freezer. Repeat this step three or four times.

THE PUDDING
700 g (1 lb 9 oz) frozen mango purée
3½ tablespoons sugar syrup (Essentials, page 240)
150 ml (5 fl oz) evaporated milk
12 g (¼ oz) gelatine leaves

In a large bowl, combine the mango purée, sugar syrup and evaporated milk and whisk well. In a separate bowl, soak the gelatine leaves in cold water for about 5 minutes until soft. Remove the leaves from the water and gently squeeze out the excess. Set aside.

Add 150 ml (5 fl oz) of the mango mixture to a small saucepan over a medium heat. When it starts simmering around the edges, add the soaked gelatine leaves and stir until the gelatine has completely dissolved. Stir this mixture back into the remaining mango mixture and whisk thoroughly. Divide the mixture among four shallow moulds, cover and refrigerate overnight.

TAPIOCA
100 g (3½ oz) tapioca pearls
375 ml (13 fl oz/1½ cups) evaporated milk

Fill a large saucepan with water and bring to the boil. Add the tapioca pearls and cook them on a rolling boil for 5–8 minutes, or until they have become soft and transparent. Drain and refresh the pearls in cold water. Put in a bowl and set aside. Just before you're ready to serve, add the evaporated milk, stirring well to combine.

THE REST
1 fresh mango, cut into 8 mm (⅜ inch) cubes
100 g (3½ oz) mango 'boba' balls
150 g (5½ oz) pomelo flesh, broken up
10 sprigs baby coriander (cilantro) sprigs, to garnish

TO SERVE

Unmould the puddings onto serving plates. Spoon about 1½ tablespoons of tapioca on top of each pudding, followed by 1 tablespoon of mango cubes and 1 tablespoon of mango balls. Scatter some pomelo flesh all over. Spoon about 2 tablespoons of passionfruit granita around each pudding and garnish with a few sprigs of baby coriander.

Growing up in suburban Australia during the 1980s and early 1990s meant one thing: bastardised Chinese food. It was awesome. Deep-fried ice cream is right up there with beef and black bean sauce, sweet and sour pork and sang choi bao. These dishes give me a real sense of nostalgia. As a kid, I wondered how a dessert could be as magic as deep-fried ice cream. I mean, ice cream. Deep-fried! We created our version of this dish for Mr Wong by giving it three textures. The ice cream is wrapped in sponge and then given a crunchy crust. The butterscotch sauce too, is our own take. The saltiness cuts the sweetness and gives it a flavour contrast. Deep-fried ice cream is one of those dishes nearly everyone has some kind of recollection of, so we felt we had a duty to respond to that (and not let the memory down).

DEEP-FRIED
ICE
CREAM

DEEP-FRIED ICE CREAM
with BUTTERSCOTCH SAUCE

Serves at least 8

ICE CREAM
12 egg yolks
250 g (9 oz) caster (superfine) sugar
500 ml (17 fl oz/2 cups) milk
500 ml (17 fl oz/2 cups) thin (pouring) cream
2 vanilla beans, split, seeds scraped out

In a bowl, whisk the egg yolks and sugar until they become pale yellow and thick. Put the milk, cream, and vanilla beans and seeds in a medium saucepan over a high heat and bring to the boil. Once boiling, remove the pan from the heat and set aside for a minute to cool. Discard the vanilla beans then whisk the hot liquid, a little at a time, into the sugary yolk mixture. Strain and leave the custard to cool. Transfer to an ice-cream machine and churn following the manufacturer's instructions. Transfer to a deep container and store in the freezer.

SPONGE
6 eggs, separated
375 g (13 oz) caster (superfine) sugar
80 g (2¾ oz) butter, melted
1 tablespoon natural vanilla extract
175 g (6 oz) plain (all-purpose) flour, sifted

Preheat the oven to 170°C (325°F/Gas 3). Line two 18 x 20 cm (7 x 8 inch) slab tins with baking paper. In a bowl, whisk the egg whites with 130 g (4½ oz) of the sugar until stiff peaks form. In another bowl, whisk the egg yolks with the remaining 245 g (8¾ oz) sugar until thick and pale. Add 3½ tablespoons hot water and continue to whisk for 2 minutes. Fold in the butter and vanilla, followed by the flour and a generous pinch of salt.

Fold the egg whites into the yolk mixture in three stages, making sure you don't over-mix as you want to retain as much air in the batter as possible. Spread the batter evenly in the prepared tins. Bake side-by-side for about 10 minutes, or until risen and cooked. You can test by inserting a skewer in the middle of a sponge. If the skewer comes out dry, the sponge is cooked. If the skewer comes out a little doughy, pop the trays back in the oven for a few more minutes then retest.

Cool the sponges in their tins. Unmould them and put in the fridge for a couple of hours, uncovered, as we want them to dry out. After that time, slice the sponge into pieces about 12 cm x 5 cm x 5 mm (4½ x 2 x ¼ inch) thick.

BUTTERSCOTCH SAUCE
120 g (4¼ oz) unsalted butter
360 g (12¾ oz) soft brown sugar
420 ml (14½ fl oz/1⅔ cups) thin (pouring) cream
2 tablespoons natural vanilla extract
small pinch ice-cream stabiliser or xanthan gum

Melt the butter and sugar in a saucepan over a medium heat. Using a thermometer, bring the mixture up to 160°C (315°F). Carefully pour in the cream (it will spit) and add the vanilla and 2 teaspoons salt. Bring the mixture back to the boil and simmer for 5 minutes. Using a hand-held blender, mix in the ice-cream stabiliser/xanthan gum.

THE REST
vegetable oil, for deep-frying
100 g (3½ oz/1⅔ cups) Japanese panko crumbs
80 g (2¾ oz) shredded coconut
3 eggs

Line a 20 x 30 cm (8 x 12 inch) slab tin with baking paper and chill in the freezer. Using an ice-cream scoop, scoop balls of ice cream about 5 cm (2 inches) in diameter onto the prepared tray. This must be done really quickly as the ice cream will start to melt. Once all the balls are on the tray, return to the freezer for the ice cream to harden, preferably overnight. They can stay in the freezer for up to 14 days before crumbing and frying them.

An hour or so before you want to eat the ice cream balls, wrap each one up using 2 pieces of sponge. They should almost resemble tennis balls because of the way the pieces of sponge lie. Make sure every bit of ice cream surface area is covered with a bit of sponge – if there are holes, tear small pieces of sponge and use them to plug the gaps. Put the sponge-covered ice cream balls back in the freezer to harden up again.

Fill a deep-fryer or large heavy-based saucepan one-third full with oil and heat to 180°C (350°F) or until a cube of bread dropped into the oil turns golden in 15 seconds. In a bowl, mix the panko crumbs and coconut together. In another bowl beat the eggs with 2½ tablespoons water. Working quickly, remove the ice-cream balls from the freezer 2 or 3 at a time, dip each ball in the beaten egg and then coat evenly in the crumbs. Drop them straight into the deep-fryer. Fry each batch for 30 seconds, or until the outside is golden. Drain on paper towel. Spoon two tablespoons of butterscotch sauce into each serving bowl and pop a deep-fried ice-cream ball on top. Serve immediately!

HONG HACKS
Ice cream: If you can't make your own ice cream use any ice cream you like... just make sure that once you have shaped it into balls, they are frozen super hard, otherwise they won't survive the deep-frying process.

Sauce: If butterscotch sauce isn't your thing, feel free to use any topping you like. The classic Australian Chinese restaurant usually offered raspberry or chocolate sauce as options.

Sponge: Not a baker? Buy it.

DEEP-FRIED ICE CREAM

Using an ice-cream scoop, scoop balls of ice cream about 5 cm (2 inches) in diameter onto a tray or flat dish. This must be done really quickly as the ice cream will start to melt. Once all the balls are on the tray, return to the freezer for the ice cream to harden, preferably overnight. They can stay in the freezer for up to 14 days before crumbing and frying them.

Wrap each one up using 2 pieces of sponge. They should almost resemble tennis balls because of the way the pieces of sponge lie. Make sure every bit of ice cream surface area is covered with a bit of sponge – if there are holes, tear small pieces of sponge and use them to plug the gaps.

Working quickly, remove the ice-cream balls from the freezer 2 or 3 at a time, dip each ball in the beaten egg and then coat evenly in the crumbs.

CHAPTER FIVE
YOUNGER YEARS

I didn't grow up wanting to be a chef. Truth be told, I wasn't really sure what I wanted to do. I went to school in the north-western suburbs of Sydney and I wasn't the brightest kid at school. And from year 10 or so, I probably smoked too much pot for my own good. We weren't bad kids, but the other groups called us 'The Hards', which was hilarious because we came from a fairly exclusive north shore private school... hardly the depths of the ghetto. We stayed out all night and went to raves, and a few of us started doing graffiti at the same time. A few friends ended up sticking with it and becoming artists, but that wasn't on the cards for me – my mum had other ideas.

My mum fell into owning a restaurant in the centre of Sydney's Vietnamese community in Cabramatta around the time I turned eleven. When I say 'fell', she really didn't see it coming. She had taken me and my sister Rebecca to Vietnam for the very first time, and our other sister Francoise and our dad stayed at home to work. While we were away discovering the joys of walking around early morning Saigon, learning how to eat river snails, fertilised duck eggs and freshly steamed rice noodles from road stalls, Dad called Mum and said, 'Angie, we bought a restaurant.' It was a massive surprise, considering she was an interpreter by profession and neither of them had a background in restaurants or cooking.

So when we got home, Mum eventually quit her interpreting gig and found herself in the middle of John Street. It was the most densely populated strip of Vietnamese restaurants in Sydney, and she was cooking on it. She had to draw on all of her memories of growing up as a kid in Saigon, watching, smelling, tasting, to make it work. The one thing she knew she didn't want was to be the same as everyone else on the strip. So she started using better produce; butter lettuce instead of iceberg, making things lighter and fresher, adding her own (not so authentic) twists to sauces and dressings. Critic Terry Durack reviewed her in 1995. It was one of the first 'ethnic' restaurants to be reviewed in the *Sydney Morning Herald*, and suddenly people started travelling all the way from inner Sydney to eat her food.

Around the same time, my dad's parents migrated to Australia from Vietnam, which was great for us because my grandma was an amazing cook and we got to go to her house every Sunday for dinner. The French colonisation of Vietnam meant she knew how to make her own saucisson, pâté and head cheese. Her profiteroles though, were decidedly half French, half Vietnamese. She'd make technically perfect choux pastry, and then fill them with durian flavoured crème patissiere.

The Sunday meal would start with her famous charcuterie and baguette, then *Bo Hyung Nyam* – beef cooked in a vinegar-based steamboat, with pineapple, onions and lemongrass. The dish was served with rice paper, a heap of fresh herbs and fermented anchovy sauce. But the meal would always end with those profiteroles.

Towards the end of high school, my mum had a fairly good inkling that I wasn't going to do that well academically. She asked me if I'd be interested in going to the hotel school… 'Why don't you be a chef?' My parents loved food of all kinds, and around the end of high school, on special occasions like birthdays, we were allowed to choose a restaurant that our whole family would like to go to. Rockpool, Salt and Claude's were some of my first memories of fine dining. I remember Tim Pak Poy coming out from the kitchen at Claude's and saying hello. I think that sense of hospitality made a bigger impression on me than I probably knew at the time.

I also think being stoned all the time gave me a really good appreciation of food and experimenting with it. I loved the supermarket. I'd go there and be mesmerised by the packaging and the products, especially in the frozen aisle. I'd look for anything that would be awesome deep-fried… pizza pockets were gold.

My mum was constantly working when my sisters and I were growing up, so a lot of the time we were left to our own devices. When she did cook, it was a huge treat. Huge pots of oxtail soup and ragu (recipes learnt from when she was in France), or vats of pho that we loved and would eat for every meal for days on end. Coming home from school and smelling pho or *mi vi tiem* stock that had been simmering for a whole day always made us happy. Once a week, Mum would leave pork ribs or chicken wings marinating in the fridge in fish sauce, sugar, golden syrup (an Angie-ism), lemongrass and garlic and go to work. We'd get home from school, grill them and eat them with rice, cucumber, tomato and Maggi seasoning.

Whether it was because of that ritual or not, I started experimenting with marinating: chicken, fish, steak, whatever I could find in the kitchen. My first success was when my parents bought a barbecue and I marinated steak with chopped garlic and mixed dried herbs and cooked it for them. My family was like, 'That's the best steak we've ever had!' I'm still not sure if they were serious or joking, but my next mountain to climb was a roasted leg of lamb.

I got accepted into cooking school before my final results were in, and by that time, I'd basically mentally checked out because I knew where I was going after school. I started cooking school in January 2001, straight after I finished year 12.

To be honest, I found the initial stages of cooking school a bit boring. It was the French classical training method, which itself was pretty interesting, but on Fridays we had to work in the hotel kitchen. It was soul destroying. Continuous chopping of scallions for eight hours on end, with no explanation of what would happen to them next, or even an opportunity to taste the final dish. So I stopped going. The school said, 'If you don't go to cross training, you can't get a job in the hotel.' I remember thinking that was fine, because the last thing I wanted to do was work in a hotel. I wanted to work in a restaurant.

And that was it. If I knew nothing else at that stage, I knew I wanted to work in a restaurant, and that I definitely didn't want to end up working in a hotel brigade somewhere. The best thing about cooking school was that we got to go to Thailand. It really opened my eyes to the cuisine, as I'd never really experienced it properly before. I'd get up early before the scheduled breakfast and walk around and

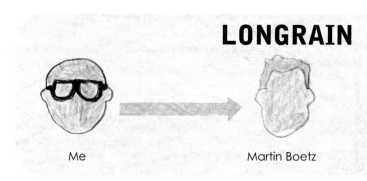

LONGRAIN

Me → Martin Boetz

look for street food. I'd watch women making *pad see ew* and grilling pork balls by the side of the road – that trip really made me start to appreciate Thai cuisine.

At the end of my cooking school training, Mum said, 'When you finish, I can ask Martin Boetz if he might have a job for you.' Longrain was one of the hottest restaurants in Sydney and Martin Boetz was known for making Thai food THE cuisine of the moment. Mum (who has a habit of becoming friends with everyone she meets) had gotten to know Martin through his friend Lindy Thompson, who came out to eat at Mum's restaurant.

So I finished cooking school with a High Distinction and I got the job as a first-year apprentice at Longrain. I was nervous as hell, rocking up with my red toolbox (the hallmark of a bonafide hotel school graduate newbie) and neck scarf. Luckily Joe Campbell, one of the sous chefs, took me under his wing. He'd trained with the legendary Phillip Searle and was best mates with another chef, Brent Savage, who I would eventually work for.

My training at Longrain was fundamental to the skills I rely on today. There, I learnt how to cut things as finely as possible. Also, Joe would always say 'A good chef should know exactly how much of each ingredient is in the cool room at all times.' I would quiz him just to make sure he really knew. That's the sign of a great chef – doing a better job than anyone else, if you're going to preach it.

It was also there that I learnt the importance of constantly tasting everything. Because every curry was cooked to order, you'd have to fry off the paste, taste it, season it, taste it, add the ingredients, the stock, the coconut milk, sugar, taste it… by the end, you'd have a screwed-up palate, but the habit was invaluable. From dressings to frying eschalots, I learnt how to formally identify the flavour elements I grew up just accepting as a kid. Sweet, salty, sour, bitter, spicy – how to make these balance in a dish is the foundation of Asian cooking. My food philosophy today is about big flavours, not subtlety, and I still reference Thai food for its potency, its ability to punch you in the face.

After a year of working at Longrain, I had learnt a lot. My knife skills were immaculate, thanks to the level of competition among the chefs. Someone would walk past your station and throw super thinly sliced lime leaves at your wall to see how many would stick. It'd be like BOOM, check that out! I was itching to get out there though, to try other things.

I ended up at Pello under Thomas Johns at the height of the Franglish explosion in Sydney. French-influenced British food cooked by white, angry men was all the rage. It was the era of Banc, which turned out amazing contributors to the Australian restaurant industry, like Justin North, Warren Turnbull and Colin Fassnidge. I had absolutely no idea what I was doing there. The culture and the techniques seemed so

PELLO

Thomas Johns

MARQUE

Mark Best   Tony Gibson   Pasi Petanen

foreign to me. They asked me to slice a cucumber and I immediately went into ninja Longrain mode. They were like, 'Whoah... that's *too* thin. Can you do it *thicker*?' I think they liked me as an apprentice because I was the kid with mad knife skills who didn't ask stupid questions and worked with a sense of urgency.

Thomas was such a generous boss. He'd save up all of our tips and then take us out to eat somewhere amazing because he believed we needed to taste and experience what the best in Sydney were doing. It also felt like we had a family. It was at Pello that I discovered that I really liked working in the pastry section. It was pretty rare for a second-year apprentice to work all stations, but Thomas allowed me to. He'd also allow us to have a creative outlet by coming up with a new amuse bouche every day. That kind of freedom and trust is rare. I was once allowed to create a dessert for the menu. It involved passionfruit fried ice cream with pineapple, poached in kaffir lime syrup. It was a dish where I tried to incorporate all of my training at Longrain with the European techniques I was being exposed to at Pello. When it received a mention in a review in the paper, I felt pretty good about it. Somebody thought something I made was worth telling people about, and that was thrilling.

Hip hop made our relationship. Thomas and I became good mates in the end because we found something outside of food that we both really liked. He'd also give me lists of restaurants he thought I should try and he even helped me get a trial for a job at Marque.

Arriving at Marque was one of the toughest times in my cooking career. I had never worked in fine dining before and it was full on. I had learnt by then that the best way to get a job as an apprentice was to keep your mouth shut, do what you're told (to the letter) and do it as fast and as perfectly as you possibly could. So I got the job, but then the real work began.

Owner and executive chef Mark Best's sous chef Tony Gibson had just arrived straight from Gordon Ramsay's, aka The Mothership (of Franglish cuisine). The pursuit of perfection was borderline insanity and the pressure nearly overwhelmed me.

Marque had two hats. Mark wanted three. This put an incredible amount of pressure on the kitchen. The first time I got a bollocking from Besty was a massive blow. After being nurtured at Pello, I found myself in a place with nowhere to hide. He was omnipresent and I feel privileged to have cooked there at a time when there was so much hunger for perfection and recognition.

He was hard on us, hurling constant abuse. He'd plate up and say, 'That's why I'm number 1. And you're number 53,263.' It wasn't all too serious though; he could take it if you dished it back (within reason). You wouldn't want to screw with that guy though.

MOOG

Brent Savage

TETSUYA'S

Tetsuya   Dave Pegrum   Martin Benn

The first few months I worked there I was filled with dread on the daily. I'd get off the train at Central Station and I got heavier with every step I took up the hill towards Marque. One day, it was just me and Besty in the kitchen and I had to plate up all the entrées and mains while he was on the stoves. Between the two of us, we did 30 covers that night... and I didn't get yelled at. I finally felt like I might deserve to be there, and might learn something. It's times like these that I really cherish from the experience. Being under the tutelage of someone like Besty, one on one, I learnt a lot. There, I cultivated more subtle techniques; how to poile (baste with butter), how to refine my technique and appreciate the art of being gentle. Besty's time with Alain Passard made him great at finding the perfect technique for every protein.

This was a time before sous vide. A time of low oven temps, trays of water and miles of plastic wrap. Because of it, I learnt how to cook properly; to be methodical and develop a hyper attention to detail.

Tony left as head chef and Pasi Petanen came on board. It was the first time I'd seen Besty listen to ideas from other chefs – the mutual respect and collaboration of ideas was great to watch.

I distinctly remember one of the first big nights I was allowed on the sauce section. It was Pasi's section (also the hardest one to work) and it's a test of whether a chef will make it or fail spectacularly. A whole heap of dockets for orders came through and I very nearly lost it, and Besty was yelling at me, telling me to get off and get Pasi back on. It was the first time in my career I pushed back and made them let me work through it. I managed to pull through to the end of service and to this day, I still feel a huge sense of achievement in making it through that night. I remember thinking, 'I can do this shit.'

After doing all sections at Marque, I felt it was time to move on again. I don't think Besty took it very well, and he sent me to his other restaurant Moog, headed up by Brent Savage. Brent and I worked together for the last month of my apprenticeship and kept in touch when it was over.

Then, I had the great idea of asking for a job at Tetsuya's. I don't advise it, but on my first day as a fully qualified chef, I walked up to the front gates of Tetsuya's and rang the bell. Somehow, I got let in and started knocking on the huge, heavy front doors, hoping they would open. A car pulled into the driveway and out came Vicki Wild, Tetsuya's PA at the time and now co-owner of Sepia. After receiving a total ear bashing for turning up unannounced, she left me in the bar while she went to get Dave Pegrum, the head chef at the time. He seemed pretty cool! He looked at my CV, looked at me and then said, 'OK cool, so come in for a trial.'

BENTLEY

Luke Powell   Darren Robertson   Phil Wood   Jowett Yu

Brent Savage

Tetsuya's immediately struck me as being such a well-oiled machine. Twenty chefs, divided up into teams, with four chefs standing around each station. One would put on the chives. Another would put on the protein. Another would add the sauce, the other would wipe the plate. An order was called. Everyone would repeat it in unison. 'Oui chef, table 90, 2 oysters.'

The greatest thing about doing a trial at Tetsuya's is that you get to eat the whole degustation in the kitchen. It was the first time I'd ever experienced Japanese flavours executed with French technique. Tets is the master of (dare I say it) 'fusion' (OK, I said it). After my trial, I got the job. That time in the history of Tetsuya's formed the basis of some of the strongest friendships I have today. Luke Powell, Phil Wood, Martin Benn, Darren Robertson… and of course my co-conspirator and close mate Jowett Yu.

Working at Tetsuya's is the ultimate pursuit of perfection. But for the first month, it is also super depressing. Every time you think you've done something well, you have 19 other chefs telling you that you did it wrong. Tets wasn't in the kitchen much, but when he was, it was like, 'God has entered the building.' Ideally, he'd taste what you'd done and walk away (that's when you knew you'd done a good job). Again, I learnt the importance of tasting at every stage. It sounds so simple, but I don't think enough chefs remember to do it.

Perfection is at once simple and complex. I remember there being a dessert: a single slice of musk melon. Every single melon we got in had to be sliced open and tasted. If it wasn't good enough, the whole melon was thrown out. That's how you get to be #4 restaurant in the world.

Martin Benn had returned as head chef at Tetsuya's and on the night of the announcement of the World's Top 50 Restaurant awards in London, he called everyone into the kitchen. He said, 'I just want to say, we're the 4th best restaurant in the world. But we have to keep it up. So if you don't want to work here, you can f*** off right now. This is no time to slouch. But if you are staying, make sure you're the very best you can be.'

And that's how it was. In the face of absolute perfection, friendships became important at Tets. We needed time to blow off steam and be less serious. Phil, Luke, Jow and I became good mates. We'd go out together to eat, talk about what was going on in food around the world in places like Spain and France, and generally get drunk. Good times.

At the end of my year at Tetsuya's, I went to join Bentley Restaurant + Bar, which Brent Savage was about to open with sommelier Nick Hildebrandt. Ben Milgate and Elvis Abrahanowicz were on board as co-sous chefs and I would come on as chef de partie. I ended up as sous chef by default because Ben and Elvis had the opportunity to open their own restaurant, Bodega.

BEST FRIEND

Louis Tikaram

WIFE

Rara

DAUGHTER

Namira

Wylie Dufresne

In my new role as sous chef, I admit I was a total bastard. I'd come from a few incredible restaurants and felt that doing my time meant I could be a prick to the juniors in the same way I experienced. I also wanted to show Brent that I was loyal to his vision. Even Brent told me to ease up a bit.

The food at Bentley was decidedly molecular. I hate that term now, but it really was. Spain was the capital of the food world and Ferran Adria was its king. Brent had staged in Barcelona and the techniques and flavours he brought back with him were incredible. Spherification! Methylcellulose! Agar agar! Pacojets! They were hardcore drugs and we were all addicted.

Marque was hard, but Bentley was equally difficult in a different way. Being more senior meant I had to teach people things and lead by example. We were also open for lunch and dinner five days a week, which meant doubles every day. Sometimes lunch service would flow straight into dinner and we ended up coining it 'mono service'. It was there that I met Louis Tikaram (who decided to rename 'mono service' 'ballz deep'), who started as an apprentice and became my best mate. It was also where I met my wife, Rara.

Rara had moved from Indonesia to Sydney to start at Le Cordon Bleu. She was a total princess. She ate at Bentley at least once a week and one of the waiters, Paddy, used to go over and talk to these 'two hot Indo girls'. He walked into the kitchen one night and said, 'One of those chicks wants to work here.' Brent went out and brought her into the kitchen. Brent said to us, 'This is Rara, she's starting with us next week.' And I remember checking her out and thinking 'Nice'. Typical chefs being pervs. Louis said to her, 'You from Indo? Bring gado gado.' The next day, at 8 am, she turned up with gado gado for the kitchen.

I remember asking her if she had a boyfriend, and she told me her boyfriend of eight years lived in Jakarta. I thought to myself 'Challenge accepted.'

A little while later, we got together and the rest is history. We have a daughter named Namira, and she's pretty much the centre of our universe.

Back at Bentley, the restaurant was awarded *Sydney Morning Herald* Best New Restaurant and two hats, which was amazing. It finally gave us and the junior chefs some recognition for all the hard work we'd endured during opening year and, as the sous chef, I felt particularly proud. I decided I wanted to reapply for the Josephine Pignolet Young Chef of the Year award. It's a scholarship I'd applied for and missed out on a year or so before. I think the first time around, I was too arrogant, too sure of myself. This time, I'd seen and done a few things that gave me a better sense of humility. I can't be sure, but I feel like that's why they gave the award to me that year.

LOTUS

Lauren Murdoch

MERIVALE

Frank Roberts   Justin Hemmes

Winning the JP award means you receive not only approval by the industry's greats, but money to travel and stage at the world's top restaurants. All I wanted to do was go to New York and work at wd~50. At the time, Wylie Dufresne was doing really interesting things with hydrocolloids, and was one of The Bentley Bar's greatest influences.

Originally, I planned to get there and apply for sponsorship so I could stay for a few years. In the end, I decided to stay for two months. I found out when I got there that wd~50 didn't sponsor. Two Aussies worked there, and one of them, Glen Goodwin, had been living there illegally for 10 years. Staging can be amazing, but also a bit tough until you earn your stripes. The kitchen crew would give me so much shit. 'Do you baptise your babies in Foster's? You're Australian and you've never been to Outback Steakhouse?'

Wylie was really cool from the start though. You could ask him questions and he would explain the answer like a true scientist. He'd take the time to break a response down and discuss it objectively, which for a guy in his position was a huge honour to a kid from Sydney.

It was in New York that I discovered the love affair I never knew I had… burgers. If there's ever a place to fall in love with them, it's in the Big Apple. More on that elsewhere.

When I returned to Sydney I worked at Bentley for a bit, until Frank Roberts, a guy I'd known since I was a second-year apprentice at Pello, called me. He'd been managing Est at the time and had recently become the Merivale restaurant group's group restaurant manager. He used to come to Bentley for snacks, so I knew him pretty well. The call was to invite me to lunch at Est. I had no idea what it was about, I just knew I was going to dine at Est for free, so I was pumped. For the record, if anyone invites you to Est, even if it's to break up with you, take it.

Over lunch, Frank told me that Lauren Murdoch, the chef at Lotus, which, like Est, was owned by Merivale, was planning to leave. Everyone loved her food there, but she was moving on to start Ash Street Cellar. He asked me if I wanted to apply for the job. I told him I'd think about it, but internally I was over the moon.

The day of my tasting trial was tough. Justin is almost always late because he schedules about a thousand meetings a day. And when you do get his attention, you have about 45 minutes before he has to leave. I'd prepped, expecting him to turn up at 12. He kept calling to say he was running late. In the end, he was three hours late and I had 35 minutes to cook him 12 courses. It was one of the hardest services of my life, but when I walked out, everyone stood up and started clapping. I knew I'd found people who appreciated my food. In the years since I started with Merivale in 2008, they've been huge believers in what I'm capable of and have continued to push me to explore what's possible. As a chef, you can hope for no greater support.

Tonkotsu ramen is one of my favourite comfort foods. It's sticky and gelatinous and rich. It really became an obsession when me and my friends tried Gumshara Ramen in a food court in Chinatown called Eating World (my kind of world). I nicknamed it The Chronic – I tweeted once 'I just tried the tonkotsu ramen at Eating World... it was so chronic' – and the name stuck. People started calling it The Chronic and the rest is history. From that point onwards, Jow and I wanted to try tonkotsu ramen anywhere that made it. As part of a [TOYS] Collective dinner we did at Ms G's, Jow wanted to make his own version. He bought a heap of books from Japan, studied like a demon and made his own version from those ideas. The pork back fat is the key – it emulsifies with the bones and gives you that rib sticking, unctuous texture. This recipe takes a bit of work and your house will smell pretty porky, but I can't see how that's a bad thing.

TONKOTSU

RAMEN

TONKOTSU RAMEN

Serves 6

DAY 1

RAMEN STOCK
3 kg (6 lb 12 oz) pork bones
1–2 pork trotters, split lengthways (ask your butcher)
1 boiler chicken
20 g (¾ oz) dried shiitake mushrooms, tied in a muslin (cheesecloth) bag
250 g (9 oz) pork back fat, cut into 2 cm (¾ inch) cubes
1 brown onion
½ bunch spring onions (scallions)

Put the pork bones, trotters and boiler chicken in a very large stockpot. Top with cold water and bring to the boil.

As soon as the water reaches a rolling boil, take the pot off the heat and drain everything into a clean sink. Wash everything really well under running water. Be sure to remove the grey coagulated blood and white protein from the crevices and watch for dirt between the toes of the trotters. Wash out the inside of the boiler chicken as well. This step is really important because it will mean the difference between a brownish stock and a beautiful milky one.

Clean the pot you've just used really well, removing any scum and debris. Return the pork bones, trotters and boiler chicken to the pot, add the bag of dried shiitakes and cover with water. Turn the heat up to high and bring to a rolling boil. Start skimming off all the scum that rises to the surface. Turn the heat down to medium to maintain a steady rolling boil. This will help any fat to emulsify with the stock.

After 5 hours, remove the boiler chicken and shiitakes. Keep the stock bubbling along, taking notice of the water level (if it becomes too low, top up with hot water).

At the eighth hour, add the pork fat to the stock. Reduce the heat: you want the stock simmering enough to melt the pork fat, but not at the rolling boil you had earlier. An hour later, peel and roughly dice the onion, and trim the spring onions. Add these to the stock, then turn the heat up to medium–high.

At the 10-hour mark, the bones should be calcified, which makes them very brittle. Bash the bones with a big wooden spoon or a solid wooden rolling pin until they break. Be careful not to burn yourself with the splashing stock. Once you have done this, scrape the bottom of the pot as the bones might catch.

Strain the stock into a large bowl through a fine sieve, removing all the meat and bone pieces. Cover and refrigerate to use the next day.

MASTERSTOCK BRAISED PORK BELLY CHASHU
5 litres (175 fl oz/20 cups) Chinese masterstock (Essentials, page 234)
1 kg (2 lb 4 oz) piece of pork belly
500 ml (17 fl oz/2 cups) cooking sake
300 ml (10½ fl oz) mirin
6 eggs, at room temperature

Pour the masterstock into a large pot and bring to the boil. Roll the pork belly and secure it tightly with butcher's twine. Add it to the masterstock and braise it for up to 4 hours, or until soft. Add the sake and mirin, then remove from the heat and leave for the pork belly to cool in the stock. Once the stock has cooled sufficiently, cover and refrigerate.

Bring a saucepan of water to the boil, then gently lower the eggs into the water. Set a timer for 5 minutes. As soon as the timer goes off, remove the eggs and plunge them into a bowl of iced water to stop the cooking process. After a few minutes, peel the eggs, and add them to the refrigerated masterstock pot with the pork belly.

RAMEN DASHI
25 g (1 oz) dried kombu
15 g (½ oz) dried anchovies
20 g (¾ oz) bonito flakes (katsuoboshi)

DASHI TARE
15 g (½ oz) dried kombu
180 ml (6 fl oz) white soy sauce
125 ml (4 fl oz/½ cup) soy sauce
125 ml (4 fl oz/½ cup) mirin
100 g (3½ oz) salt

Fill two 3-litre (105 fl oz/12 cup) containers with 2.5 litres (87 fl oz/10 cups) cold water. In one container, soak the kombu for the ramen dashi. In the other container, soak the kombu for the dashi tare. Cover, label which is which and refrigerate both containers overnight.

DAY 2

RAMEN DASHI

Pour the contents of the container into a large saucepan. Heat over a medium heat and, as the water starts to simmer, remove the kombu and set it aside. Add the dried anchovies to the simmering water, turn down the heat and let the mixture simmer gently for 30 minutes. Remove from the heat. Add the bonito flakes and let them sink to the bottom. Strain the solids from the dashi and put them aside with the reserved kombu, as you will need these for the dashi tare.

DASHI TARE

Pour the contents of the container into a large saucepan. Bring to a simmer over a medium heat. Add the ingredients you just strained from the ramen dashi and gently simmer for 30 minutes. Strain, discarding the solids. Whisk in the soy sauces, mirin and salt. The resulting mixture is the seasoning soy you'll need for the ramen.

NOODLES
2 teaspoons bottled lye water
675 g (1 lb 8 oz/4½ cups) plain (all-purpose) flour

Combine the lye water with 310 ml (10¾ fl oz/ 1¼ cups) filtered tap water to make kansui water. Add the kansui water and the flour to the bowl of an electric mixer or food processor with a dough hook attachment. Mix until everything comes together and forms a dough. You can also do this by hand.

If the dough feels a little dry and brittle, add a bit more water. On a lightly floured bench, roll out the dough to a smooth thick(ish) rectangle. Fold it over and put in a zip-lock bag, making sure all the air pockets are squeezed out. Leave in the fridge for 1 hour to rest. This step is really important because the dough will soften and become pliable.

If you have a pasta machine, roll the dough out into thin sheets and cut into thin noodles. Alternatively roll it out as thin as you can by hand and slice into noodles that way.

THE REST
½ bunch spring onions (scallions), sliced into thin rounds
3 tablespoons sesame seeds, to garnish

Remove the ramen stock from the fridge. All of the fat will have risen to the top and solidified, but don't be afraid of this – the fat is really important to the flavour of the stock and texture of the dish, so leave it in. Put the stock in a large saucepan and bring to the boil.

Remove the pork belly chashu and eggs from the masterstock. Slice the pork thinly, and let it come to room temperature. Cut each egg in half lengthways.

Season the hot stock by mixing it with some of the ramen dashi and dashi tare. The ratio is purely a personal thing, so add each one slowly and stop when you've reached your own balance. The dashi adds umami, and will dilute the thick gelatinous pork stock, whereas the tare will add seasoning to the soup.

TO SERVE

Cook the noodles in rapidly boiling water until al dente – they should have a firm bite. Drain the noodles and transfer to a large serving bowl. Top with the pork chashu and ladle in the hot stock. Top with the eggs and spring onions, scatter with sesame seeds and then serve at once.

HONG HACKS
Don't want to make the ramen noodles, just buy 'em.

Sub out the chashu, with sliced roasted pork belly from your local Chinese BBQ restaurant.

I think tonkotsu ramen is actually pretty easy to make. It takes a long time, but the steps are relatively simple. These photographed steps do help though, because it's important to know what success looks like at each stage when you do it for the first time.

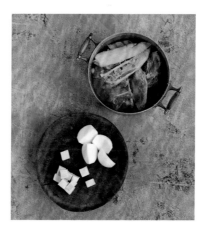

The raw ingredients.

After a while, all the meat will fall off the bones as they start to calcify.

The seasoning process: filtered stock, dashi and tare.

Braise the pork belly in the masterstock until the fat is meltingly soft.

Charshu, cooled and sliced.

Make the noodles in small batches so they don't dry out.

Dust the noodles with extra flour so they don't stick together.

I can't live without noodle soups… they are my everything. Take a nourishing broth and some protein, add noodles and you have one of the most satisfying things you can eat. From Japanese ramen to Malaysian laksa and *har mee*, Cambodian *hu tieu nam vang* and Cantonese wonton noodle soup, every Asian country has at least one iconic noodle soup. For me, the king of all noodle soups is Bún bò Huê, a spicy beef concoction that originated in Hue, central Vietnam. The broth hits all areas of your palate, fish sauce adds umami and the textures of braised pork hock, trotters and slippery noodles seal the deal.

BÚN BÒ HUÊ

Serves 6–8

THE STOCK

5 kg (11 lb 4 oz) pork bones

2 kg (4 lb 8 oz) beef bones

2 pork hocks

3 pig's trotters, halved lengthways

2 beef shins

6 lemongrass stems, pale part only, roughly chopped and bashed

1 pineapple, peeled, roughly chopped

2 onions, halved

10 garlic cloves

2 tablespoons shrimp paste

400 ml (14 fl oz) fish sauce

500 g (1 lb 2 oz) caster (superfine) sugar

3¾ tablespoons salt

Put the pork and beef bones, hocks, trotters and shins in a heavy-based stockpot and cover with cold water. Put over a high heat and bring to the boil. Once it has reached boiling point, remove from the heat and drain into a clean sink, discarding the water. Wash the bones and meat under running water to remove impurities, and wash out the inside of the pot.

Return the bones to the pot, then place the hocks, trotters and shins on top of them. Cover with cold water and bring to the boil. Skim off any scum that rises to the surface, then add the lemongrass, pineapple, onions and garlic. Simmer for 2½ hours.

Remove the hocks, trotters and shins and leave to cool. Keep simmering the stock for another 3 hours. When the pork hocks are cool enough to handle, remove the meat from the bone in two pieces and slice thinly, about 2 mm (¹⁄₁₆ inch) in thickness. Cut each piece of trotter through the joints into 3–4 bits then slice the shins into the same thickness as the hocks. Set the trotter, hock and shin meats aside.

Drain the stock and add the shrimp paste, fish sauce, caster sugar and salt. These seasoning quantities are just a guideline. You may need to add more or less fish sauce, sugar or salt to get the right balance. Add a little more shrimp paste if you like a more pungent stock and remember to taste the stock and adjust to suit your palate.

LEMONGRASS CHILLI OIL

30 g (1 oz) annatto seeds
250 ml (9 fl oz) vegetable oil
1½ tablespoons chilli oil
2 lemongrass stems, white part only, very finely chopped
2 spring onions (scallions), very finely chopped
4 garlic cloves, very finely chopped
1 teaspoon chilli flakes
½ tablespoon salt
½ tablespoon sugar
1 tablespoon fish sauce

Put the annatto seeds and vegetable oil in a small saucepan and heat over a medium heat. The annatto will begin to colour the oil. Continue cooking until the oil develops a deep orange colour, about 4 minutes. Drain and discard the annatto.

Put the annatto-infused oil in a wok and add the chilli oil. Put over a medium heat and add the lemongrass, spring onions, garlic and chilli flakes. Fry the lot for about 3 minutes until the spring onions are softened and fragrant. Season with the salt, sugar, and fish sauce and adjust to taste. Store unstrained in a sterilised jar.

THE REST

400 g (14 oz) thick rice vermicelli noodles
200 g (7 oz) chà lua (Vietnamese pork loaf), thinly sliced
1 red onion, thinly sliced
3 spring onions (scallions), green part only, thinly sliced
1 small handful of coriander (cilantro) leaves, roughly chopped
200 g (7 oz) purple cabbage, finely shredded
100 g (3½ oz) Chinese water spinach, finely shredded
1 small handful of round leaf mint, roughly chopped, and Vietnamese mint leaves, to garnish
lemon wedges, to serve

Cook the vermicelli in boiling water according to the packet instructions. Drain and refresh under cold running water, then set aside. Put the hock, trotter and shin meats into the stock and bring to the boil. As soon as it starts to boil, remove the pot from the heat.

TO SERVE

Put a handful of noodles in each serving bowl and top with slices of the hock, trotter and shin and chà lua. Drizzle a little lemongrass chilli oil over each dish, then add some red onions, spring onions and coriander. Pour the just-boiled broth over the top. Serve immediately, with the cabbage, water spinach, mint and lemon wedges on the side.

Everything you need to make a great Bún bò Huê stock.

Beef shin, pork hock and chà lua.

Infusing the oil with annatto seeds.

The finished seasoned oil.

> Grilled seafood is an Australian birthright. This dish takes the classic grilled prawn and pimps the umami factor with kombu butter and shellfish oil.

GRILLED KING PRAWNS
with KOMBU BUTTER

Serves 4–5 as a starter

KOMBU BUTTER
500 g (1 lb 2 oz) unsalted butter, softened
1 tablespoon onion powder
2 teaspoons garlic powder
40 g (1½ oz) shio kombu, finely chopped
2 garlic cloves, finely chopped
1½ tablespoons mirin
1 tablespoon fish sauce
½ bunch coriander (cilantro) stems, finely chopped
2 lemongrass stems, pale part only, finely chopped
1 small handful of flat-leaf (Italian) parsley leaves, finely chopped

Put the butter in the bowl of an electric mixer fitted with a whisk attachment and whip at a high speed for 10 minutes, or until it becomes pale and aerated. Reserve a big pinch of each of the chopped herbs, which will be used to garnish. Turn the mixer down to its lowest speed and add the remaining ingredients one at a time, mixing after each addition.

THE REST
10 large raw king prawns (shrimp), split in half lengthways, digestive tract removed
mixed chopped herbs from above, to garnish
2½ tablespoons shellfish oil (Essentials, page 237)
lime wedges, to serve

Preheat the oven to 250ºC (500ºF/Gas 9). Lay the prawns on a baking tray, shell side down. Season with salt and put in the oven for 2½ minutes. Remove the tray from the oven and spoon a thick layer of kombu butter on each prawn. Bake for another 2½ minutes. To serve, top each prawn with some chopped herbs and drizzle with shellfish oil. Serve with lime wedges.

This is one of my favourite soups made by my mum and is total comfort food for me. She has cooked this from as early as I can remember, and funnily enough the secret is – are you ready? – tinned asparagus. It's a clear case of fresh is not always best. The soft texture of tinned asparagus adds to the silkiness of the soup, and you also need the juice from the tin. I won't lie: I'm pretty sure Mum would have also made this soup using tinned crab once upon a time but go for the fresh stuff where possible. Mum won't judge you for using tinned crab if you're on a budget.

MUM'S CRAB and ASPARAGUS SOUP

Serves about 8

BROTH
2 litres (70 fl oz/8 cups) chicken stock (Essentials, page 236)
110 g (3¾ oz/½ cup) cup caster (superfine) sugar
150 ml (5 fl oz) fish sauce
1 tablespoon salt

THE REST
500 g (1 lb 2 oz) fresh crabmeat
600 g (1 lb 5 oz) tinned white asparagus pieces, including the juice
100 g (3½ oz) potato starch mixed with 100 ml (3½ fl oz) water to make a slurry
3 egg whites, whisked together
chopped coriander (cilantro) leaves, to garnish
1 spring onion (scallion) thinly sliced, mainly the green part, to garnish
Chinese red vinegar, to serve

For the broth, bring all the ingredients to the boil and taste for seasoning. Add more fish sauce for saltiness. Add the crabmeat and asparagus, including the asparagus juice and bring back to the boil. Slowly add the potato starch slurry in a thin stream, stirring constantly. You may not need all of the slurry – stop when you have reached your preferred consistency, keeping in mind that it will continue to thicken a little after you've stopped. It should be creamy, and coat the back of a spoon.

When you're happy with the consistency, bring the soup back to the boil. Stirring gently, slowly add the egg whites in a thin stream. This will give you the 'egg flower effect' most often seen in chicken and sweet corn soup.

Divide the soup among about eight bowls and garnish each with coriander and spring onions. Let people season to their taste with freshly ground pepper and red vinegar.

Eating small birds is one of life's true pleasures and I order this dish every time I go to Mum's restaurant. I love it because the quail skin is always super crispy, the dressing is super tasty and somehow, this dish makes me like capsicums. On an ordinary day, I do not care for capsicums, but the way this dish is prepared is a winner. Start this recipe a day ahead.

MUM'S CRISPY QUAIL

Serves 4–6

MARINATED QUAIL

2½ tablespoons salt
125 ml (4 fl oz/½ cup) Knorr Liquid Seasoning
1 tablespoon finely grated ginger
1 spring onion (scallion), finely chopped
100 ml (3½ fl oz) dry sherry
150 g (5½ oz/⅔ cup) caster (superfine) sugar
1 teaspoon ground white pepper
6 quails, quartered
175 g (6 oz) potato starch
vegetable oil, for deep-frying

For the marinade, whisk together the salt, Knorr Liquid Seasoning, ginger, spring onion, sherry, sugar and white pepper in a large bowl. When combined, add the quail pieces, turning them through the marinade to coat. Cover the bowl with plastic wrap and refrigerate for at least 2 hours, but ideally for 24 hours.

CAPSICUM SALSA

1 red capsicum (pepper), finely diced
1 green capsicum (pepper), finely diced
1 yellow capsicum (pepper), finely diced
1½ teaspoons salt
3½ tablespoons vegetable oil
2 garlic cloves, finely chopped
1 teaspoon chilli flakes
2 teaspoons caster (superfine) sugar
watercress sprigs, to garnish
lemon cheeks, to serve

For the capsicum salsa, place the diced capsicums in a bowl, add the salt and mix well. Let the mixture rest for 1 hour then drain off the water that has leached out. Heat 1 tablespoon of the oil in a frying pan over a medium–high heat, then add the garlic and fry until golden and crispy. Add the capsicums, chilli flakes, sugar and remaining vegetable oil. Stir well, remove from the heat and set aside.

TO SERVE

The next day, add the potato starch to the marinating quail and mix everything together until the starch and marinade combine and, at the same time, coat the quail.

Fill a large wok or deep-fryer one-third full with oil and heat to 180°C (350°F) or until a cube of bread dropped into the oil turns golden in 15 seconds. Deep-fry the quail in batches for about 4 minutes each batch, or until golden and very crispy. Drain on paper towels. Transfer to a serving plate and top with the capsicum salsa and watercress sprigs and serve with lemon cheeks on the side.

I didn't want to put pho on the menu at Ms G's because I feel that everybody who loves this dish has a favourite spot to go for it, so why mess with that logic? This dish takes all the flavours I love about pho and makes something you can share (ever tried sharing noodle soup?). This dish is a bit involved but by the time you're done, you'll know how to make both a basic and seasoned pho stock (skills for life), as well as nailing this new dish. It's like pho, but lighter and fresher... think Vietnamese steak and salad.

STEAK with the FLAVOURS of PHO

Serves 3–4

SEASONED PHO STOCK
500 ml (17 fl oz/2 cups) pho broth (Essentials, page 236)
1½ teaspoons salt
1¼ tablespoons caster (superfine) sugar
1 tablespoon kombu extract (optional)
1¾ tablespoons fish sauce

Combine all the ingredients in a bowl, stirring until the sugar dissolves.

PHO JUS
500 ml (17 fl oz/2 cups) seasoned pho stock
100 g (3½ oz) kuzu (root starch) mixed with 100 ml (3½ fl oz) water to make a thick slurry

Bring the seasoned pho stock to the boil in a saucepan. Slowly add the slurry in a thin stream, whisking constantly. Stop adding the slurry when you reach an unctuous, saucy consistency (you will not need to add all the starch). Cover, set aside and keep warm.

HOISIN NUOC CHAM
200 ml (7 fl oz) nuoc cham (Essentials, page 244)
1½ tablespoons hoisin sauce
1 teaspoon Sriracha

Mix all the ingredients together in a bowl until well combined, then season to taste with salt and pepper.

THE STEAK
2 x 400 g (14 oz) rib eye on the bone

Season and grill the steaks in a frying pan or on a chargrill on high to your preferred degree of doneness (rare to medium is best in my opinion). Transfer to a plate, cover with foil and set aside to rest for 5 minutes.

SALAD
½ brown onion, very thinly sliced, soaked in water for 10 minutes
1 spring onion (scallion), green part only, thinly sliced
20 Thai basil leaves
20 coriander (cilantro) leaves
6 sawtooth coriander (cilantro) leaves, finely shredded
150 g (5½ oz) bean sprouts, blanched for 30 seconds then refreshed in iced water
1 long red chilli, thinly sliced into rounds
lemon wedges, to serve

TO SERVE

Combine the onions, spring onions, herbs, bean sprouts and chilli and drizzle with some of the hoisin nuoc cham. Cut the meat into 1 cm (½ inch) slices and arrange on a serving plate. Put the bones on the plate too. Spoon the pho jus over the meat, then top with the salad. Serve with lemon wedges and extra pho juice on the side.

> Vietnamese curry is a much milder affair than its Thai or Indian cousins. Pairing a curry with a baguette is also distinctly Vietnamese. We've used beef short ribs here, but any protein is suitable, from chicken legs and lamb shanks to beef shin and even goat.

VIETNAMESE CURRY of BEEF SHORT RIBS

Serves 6–8

CURRY PASTE
400 g (14 oz) red Asian shallots, roughly chopped
125 g (4½ oz) ginger, roughly chopped
75 g (2½ oz) fresh turmeric, roughly chopped
100 g (3½ oz) peeled garlic cloves
4 lemongrass stems, pale part only, finely chopped
250 g (9 oz) small long red chillies, roughly chopped
1 tablespoon shrimp paste
2 tablespoons Madras curry powder
2 tablespoons salt
200 ml (7 fl oz) vegetable oil
8 lime leaves

Put all the ingredients except 100 ml (3½ fl oz) of the oil and the lime leaves into the bowl of a food processer and whizz until it forms a smooth paste. Heat the remaining oil in a heavy-based saucepan over a high heat, add the paste and immediately reduce the heat to medium. Add the lime leaves, stirring constantly as the paste may catch on the bottom of the pan. Cook for about 15 minutes, or until the oil starts to separate from the paste. Taste the paste: it is cooked when it no longer tastes of raw garlic or onion.

THE REST
2.5 kg (5 lb 8 oz) beef short ribs, bone in, cut into 3 cm (1¼ inch) pieces
350 g (12 oz) curry paste (see above)
1 tablespoon Madras curry powder
700 ml (24 fl oz) seasoned pho stock (recipe, page 236)
200 ml (7 fl oz) coconut cream
2¼ tablespoons sugar

Put the beef short ribs in a heavy stockpot and cover them with cold water. Bring to the boil over a high heat then drain as soon as it reaches boiling point, discarding the water. Give the ribs a good wash to remove any bits of scum or impurities, and wash out the pot. Return the ribs to the pot, add the remaining ingredients and 500 ml (17 fl oz/2 cups) water. Give everything a stir and bring to the boil. Once the pot reaches boiling point, reduce the heat to low and simmer for 3 hours, or until the beef is tender and almost falling off the bone.

HERB SALAD
1 small handful of rice paddy herb (or mint or shiso leaves), roughly chopped
1 small handful of coriander (cilantro) leaves, roughly chopped
1 small handful of Thai basil leaves, roughly chopped
2 tablespoons nuoc cham (Essentials, page 244)

Combine the herbs in a small bowl and dress them with nuoc cham when ready to serve. Present the curry with the herb salad on the side and, ideally, a fresh Vietnamese baguette.

HONG HACKS
Nuoc cham: Buy it if you don't have time to make it.

Seasoned pho stock: Adds dimensions of flavour regular stock can't, but beef stock infused with ginger, star anise and clove will also work.

It's your steamboat and you'll steam if you want to. This list of ingredients is a guide. It's the stuff my family like to have when we eat steamboat and there are usually a lot of us. Scale up or down the amount of options according to your taste or budget. The main thing is to make sure your stock is perfect; the rest is up to you.

STEAMBOAT

Serves 6–8

SEAFOOD
15 raw king prawns (shrimp), peeled, with heads and tails left on
1 kg (2 lb 4 oz) blue mussels, washed, beards removed
1 kg (2 lb 4 oz) calamari, cleaned, saving the tentacles, tubes scored and cut into 5 cm (2 inch) pieces
20 scallops

MEAT
500 g (1 lb 2 oz) wagyu scotch fillet, thinly sliced
500 g (1 lb 2 oz) beef balls
500 g (1 lb 2 oz) chicken thigh fillets, cut into 2 cm (¾ inch) cubes and tossed with 1 teaspoon sugar, 1 tablespoon salt and 1 tablespoon sesame oil

VEGETABLES
400 g (14 oz) shiitake mushrooms, stems removed
300 g (10½ oz) enoki mushrooms, separated
150 g (5½ oz) washed chrysanthemum (tong ho) leaves, including stalks
1 bunch garlic chives, snipped into 10 cm (4 inch) lengths
3 baby bok choy (pak choy), quartered
20 fresh baby corns, halved lengthways

THE REST
1 packet konnyaku noodle bundles
500 g (1 lb 2 oz) cooked fresh egg noodles
200 g (7 oz) fried tofu puffs
5–6 litres (175–210 fl oz/20–24 cups) seasoned supreme stock (Essentials, page 235)

Arrange the seafood, meats and vegetables on their own separate platters. Have another platter for the konnyaku, egg noodles and tofu puffs. Steamboat is all about presentation, so be sure to fan everything out neatly, and on large platters so it presents like an abundant feast.

Put the supreme stock in a large pot that is wide and shallow so that everyone can keep an eye on what they're cooking. Put the pot on a portable gas burner in the middle of the table. Turn the burner on high and bring the stock to the boil.

Here comes the fun part: everybody puts what they want in the stock and cooks it themselves. Just be careful not to forget what you have put in – the seafood and wagyu beef will take less than 5 seconds.

The broth will accumulate more and more flavour from all the ingredients that are being cooked. People can make their own 'noodle soups', too, by mixing and matching ingredients.

It helps to have on hand a range of condiments so people can flavour their own bowls of broth. These are some suggested dipping sauces. Customising your own dipping sauce is the best thing about steamboat. It's the best of both worlds: communal dining that suits anyone's taste.

soy sauce
chopped fresh chilli
fish sauce
XO sauce
fresh lemons

OTHER STUFF YOU'LL NEED:
portable gas burner
a perforated ladle
a soup ladle
a couple of pairs of little tongs
chopsticks

HONG HACK
Everyone should have a bowl and a dipping sauce ramekin so they can customise their own signature dipping sauce.

ESSENTIALS

CHAPTER SIX

Most of the recipes in this book reference this Essentials list fairly heavily. I consider them to be basic artillery when it comes to Asian cooking, and they're recipes that are handy to master, too. With many of them, like XO sauce, Chinese masterstock and supreme stock, it is useful to make large batches and keep them on hand in either the fridge or freezer. If you put in the work here, many other recipes become a lot simpler.

Stock is the basis for all cooking, and broths are really my 'thing'. I just think a meal isn't complete without a good stock or broth to sip on. A masterstock is the classic liquor in Chinese cooking to braise meats. There have to be thousands of versions, but this version stems from my first year at Longrain and I've stuck with it ever since.

With most masterstock recipes, you put everything in and boil it. This one is different because we fry off the aromats until they've caramelised and released their flavours before we add liquid and boil it up: this adds real depth. A good masterstock can be kept indefinitely. You can freeze it, or you can keep it in the back of the fridge and boil it once a week to kill off the nasties (don't freak out: there are stories of 1000-year-old masterstocks out there). The masterstock we started when we opened Ms G's in 2010 is still going strong and getting better all the time.

Remember to keep replenishing your masterstock with more aromats as you go as the flavours accumulate the more it is used. The one thing you don't want to do is throw out or taint the masterstock with the wrong flavours. Try out different meats, especially secondary cuts. By poaching meat in masterstock, it's a meal made complete with just a bit of rice.

CHINESE MASTERSTOCK

Makes close to 12 litres (420 fl oz/48 cups)

8 red Asian shallots, coarsely chopped
10 garlic cloves
30 star anise
100 ml (3½ fl oz) vegetable oil
700 ml (24 fl oz) Shaoxing wine
1 kg (2 lb 4 oz) yellow rock sugar
500 ml (17 fl oz/2 cups) light soy sauce
700 ml (24 fl oz) dark soy sauce
100 g (3½ oz) cassia bark
4 Chinese cardamom pods
2 tablespoons fennel seeds
200 g (7 oz) ginger, thinly sliced
6 spring onions (scallions), roughly chopped
12 litres (420 fl oz/48 cups) water

Using a mortar and pestle and working in batches, pound the shallots, garlic and 10 of the star anise until a rough paste forms. Heat the vegetable oil in a heavy-based stockpot over medium–high heat and fry the paste until golden and crispy, about 5 minutes. Deglaze with the Shaoxing wine and then add the remaining ingredients. Bring to the boil, then lower the temperature and simmer for about 2 hours, skimming off any scum that may collect on the surface. Strain the solids out of the stock.

I don't know the origins of supreme stock, but it's also known as superior stock. What I do know is that it's the base for shark's fin soup, and as shark fins have very little flavour the dish is nothing without a really tasty stock. Supreme stock is also the basis of many other great soups, so this is a good recipe to perfect.

Supreme stock is traditionally made with jinhua ham in China, the Chinese equivalent of prosciutto, while the rest of the ingredients vary from recipe to recipe. Mr Wong's recipe uses smoked ham hocks because it creates that extra dimension of flavour. We also like to use dried shrimp and scallops to elevate the umami. Boiler chickens are fantastic to make stock with because they have a more chicken-y flavour, gained from a life of running around and eating all kinds of grubs and grains. Big flavour equals tasty stock. Jow and I came up with this recipe at Ms G's and I've used it ever since. It's a winner.

SUPREME STOCK

Makes at least 5 litres (175 fl oz/20 cups)

---

2 whole boiler chickens
2 smoked ham hocks
1 kg (2 lb 4 oz) chicken bones
500 g (1 lb 2 oz) chicken feet
100 g (3½ oz) dried shrimp
100 g (3½ oz) conpoy (dried scallops)
2 onions, peeled and halved
5 spring onions (scallions), trimmed

Put the chickens, ham hocks, chicken bones and chicken feet into a large stockpot. Cover with cold water and bring to the boil. As soon as it reaches a rolling boil, drain the ingredients into a clean sink, discarding the water. Wash the bones, hocks and chickens under running water to remove impurities and clean the pot out.

Start the process again by filling the pot with the washed chickens, hocks, bones and feet and covering with cold water. Put over a high heat and bring to the boil. Skim off any impurities that rise to the surface using a fine sieve.

Reduce the heat to low and bring to a slow simmer. Add the dried shrimp and conpoy, and the onions and spring onions. Simmer for about 8 hours, skimming occasionally. Strain and refrigerate. Can be frozen for up to a year or refrigerated for up to 4 days.

SEASONED SUPREME STOCK

Makes about 1 litre (35 fl oz/4 cups)

---

1 litre (35 fl oz/4 cups) supreme stock
1¼ tablespoons salt
1 tablespoon sugar
2 tablespoons kombu extract

Bring the stock to the boil and add the other ingredients. Taste and adjust the seasoning to your palate.

CHICKEN STOCK

Makes at least 5 litres (175 fl oz/20 cups)

---

2 kg (4 lb 8 oz) chicken bones
500 g (1 lb 2 oz) chicken feet
200 g (7 oz) ginger, thinly sliced
5 spring onions (scallions), roughly chopped

Put the chicken bones and feet into a large stockpot. Cover with cold water and bring to the boil. As soon as the water starts to boil, drain the contents of the pot into a clean sink, discarding the water. Wash the bones and feet of any impurities under running water. Clean out the stockpot, too.

Start the process again by returning the bones and feet to the pot, covering them with cold water and bringing to the boil over a high heat. Skim off any impurities that rise to the surface. After a few minutes, lower the heat to a simmer and add the ginger and spring onions. Simmer for 4 hours, skimming the surface occasionally. Remove from the heat, strain and cool.

This stock can be frozen for up to a year (it always helps to have stock on hand in the freezer), or it can be refrigerated for up to 3 days.

PHO BROTH

Makes at least 8 litres (280 fl oz/32 cups)

---

4 onions, peeled
350 g (12 oz) piece ginger, smashed but in 1 piece
5 kg (11 lb 4 oz) beef bones
2 pig's trotters
1 kg (2 lb 4 oz) beef brisket
6 spring onions (scallions)
100 g (3½ oz) Chinese cardamom
1 tablespoon cloves
100 g (3½ oz) cassia bark
100 g (3½ oz) star anise
33 x 2 cm (¾ inch) pieces licorice root

Using a pair of tongs, hold the onions and ginger over an open flame until the skins are nicely charred. Set aside.

Put the bones, trotters and brisket into a heavy-based stockpot. Cover with cold water, put over a high heat and bring to the boil. Remove from the heat and drain the meat, discarding the water.

Wash the bones and meat under running water to remove any impurities. Give the pot a good wash out, then return the bones, trotters and meat to the pot, cover with cold water and bring to the boil. Skim off any impurities, then add the charred onions and ginger, the spring onions and the spices. Simmer for 8 hours, skimming the surface often. Strain.

When cool, pour into a large container and store in the freezer, or keep in the fridge for up to 4 days.

At the restaurant we go through a lot of seafood, so it's easy to accumulate enough prawn and scampi shells to make an oil. At home, keep a plastic bag in the freezer and add to it when you cook shellfish. You can also use whole school prawns as a cheap, convenient alternative.

SHELLFISH OIL

Makes about 1.5 litres (52 fl oz/6 cups)

2 litres (70 fl oz/8 cups) grapeseed oil
1 kg (2 lb 4 oz) raw prawn (shrimp) shells
15 garlic cloves
10 star anise
200 g (7 oz) tomato paste (concentrated purée)

Put a heavy wide-based saucepan over a high heat. When hot, add 4 tablespoons of the oil. When the oil starts to smoke, add the prawn shells. Do not stir for at least 2 minutes (if you stir them straight away, a lot of the heat will be lost and the shells will start to stew rather than caramelise).

After 2 minutes you will start to smell that really appetising aroma of roasted prawns and you can stir the mix to further caramelise the shells. After about 5 minutes, the shells should have a nice deep red colour. Add the garlic and star anise, and stir in the tomato paste. Turn the heat down to medium.

Cook, stirring constantly, for about 5 minutes. Stir in the rest of the oil and turn the heat down to the lowest it can go. Simmer for 3 hours, remembering to scrape the bottom of the pan often, as the mixture will catch.

Strain everything through a fine sieve and leave the liquid to settle for 1 hour. All the sediment will sink to the bottom during this time. Strain the liquid a second time and carefully decant the mixture into a sterilised jar. Stop pouring when you reach the sediment. This sediment (which I call 'shellfish essence') can be used as a base for a shellfish sauce or dressing. You can store the shellfish oil in the fridge, covered, for up to 6 months.

This oil is used frequently in the recipes in this book. It's a good one to make and have handy in the fridge, to add a fragrant element to salad dressings or as a condiment in soups or stir-fried dishes.

GINGER OIL

Makes about 2 litres (70 fl oz/8 cups)

2 litres (70 fl oz/8 cups) grapeseed oil
1 kg (2 lb 4 oz) ginger, chopped roughly in a food processor
1 bunch spring onions (scallions), roughly chopped

Put the oil and ginger in a small saucepan over a low heat and slowly bring to the boil. Simmer for 10 minutes, stirring and scraping the bottom of the pan every 3–5 minutes as it will stick. Add the spring onions and stir through. Turn the heat off and leave the oil to infuse overnight.

The next day, strain out the solids and decant the oil into sterilised jars. When kept in the fridge, the oil should last a few months.

WHITE SOY DRESSING

Makes about 1.5 litres (52 fl oz/6 cups)

2½ tablespoons rice wine vinegar
100 g (3½ oz) caster (superfine) sugar
100 ml (3½ fl oz) light soy sauce
500 ml (17 fl oz/2 cups) water
100 ml (3½ fl oz) kombu extract
700 ml (24 fl oz) white soy sauce

Whisk all the ingredients together in a bowl until the sugar has dissolved. This dressing will keep in the fridge for up to 1 month. If you can't find kombu extract, it's fine to omit it.

This recipe makes a large batch. Good for giving away to friends… and you won't have to make another lot for a while.

XO SAUCE

Makes about 1 litre (35 fl oz/4 cups)

200 g (7 oz) dried shrimp
300 g (10½ oz) conpoy (dried scallops)
300 ml (10½ fl oz) cooking sake
1.1 litres (38½ fl oz) vegetable oil
100 g (3½ oz) bacon, finely chopped
20 g (¾ oz) garlic cloves, finely chopped
small long red chillies, finely chopped
40 g (1½ oz) salted black beans
30 g (1 oz) soft brown sugar
200 g (7 oz) fried shallots (Essentials, page 242)
3½ tablespoons chilli oil
1 tablespoon chilli flakes

Start by soaking the dried shrimp in water for 1 hour. Chop into very small pieces, then cover and set aside.

Put the conpoy in a bowl that fits inside a bamboo steamer and place over a saucepan of simmering water. Pour the sake over the conpoy, put the lid on, and steam for 2 hours. Drain, reserving the liquid. Shred the meat and set aside.

Fill a large wok or heavy-based saucepan one-third with oil and heat to 170°C (325°F/Gas 3) or until a cube of bread dropped into the oil turns golden in 20 seconds. Deep-fry the dried shrimp until they crisp up and turn bright orange. Using a small sieve, scoop the shrimp out and put them in a deep saucepan. Repeat the deep-frying process with the conpoy, frying them until they have taken on some colour. Scoop out and add to the saucepan with the shrimp.

Finally, deep-fry the bacon, garlic, fresh chilli and black beans for about 3–4 minutes, then transfer to the saucepan with the fried shrimp and conpoy.

Pour the reserved sake liquid into the pan. Turn the heat to low and cook for 5 minutes, stirring constantly. It's really important to keep stirring as the mixture can burn easily at this point. Add the brown sugar, fried shallots, chilli oil and chilli flakes. Continue cooking and stirring for another 5 minutes, or until the shallots are incorporated and the sugar has dissolved. Remove from the heat, cool a little then transfer to sterilised jars. You can store this sauce in the fridge for up to 6 months.

YUZU MAYONNAISE

Makes about 650 g (1 lb 7 oz)

---

3 egg yolks
35 ml (1¼ fl oz) tinned yuzu juice
1 teaspoon yuzukoshō
2 garlic cloves, finely grated
500 ml (17 fl oz/2 cups) grapeseed oil

Put all the ingredients except the oil into a food processor. Process until smooth. With the motor running, pour in the oil in a slow and steady stream. The mixture should start to emulsify and make a mayonnaise. Season to taste with salt.

SRIRACHA MAYONNAISE

Makes about 500 g (1 lb 7 oz)/2 cups)

---

375 g (13 oz) Japanese mayonnaise
65 g (2¼ oz) Sriracha sauce
1 tablespoon Knorr Liquid Seasoning

In a large bowl combine all the ingredients, whisking until incorporated. Store in a squeezie bottle in the fridge. Keeps for a long time.

SUGAR SYRUP

Makes 1.75 litres (61 fl oz/7 cups)

---

1 kg (2 lb 4 oz) sugar
1 litre (35 fl oz/4 cups) water

Put both the sugar and water in a saucepan over a high heat. Bring to a boil, stirring to ensure the sugar has completely dissolved. Cool, transfer to a container with a lid and keep refrigerated.

SLOW-COOKED EGGS

6 eggs, at room temperature

Put a plate in the bottom of a large saucepan. Fill the pan with water, clip on a cooking thermometer and bring the temperature to 63°C (113°F) over a medium heat.

Gently lower in the eggs. Keep an eye on the temperature of the water, as you want the eggs to cook for 1 hour at a constant of about 63°C (113°F). A degree or two above or below won't kill you, but try to find the temperature sweet spot on your stove. It might help if your saucepan sits part-way off the heat. Have some ice on hand in case the temperature spikes and add ice cubes one by one until the temperature lowers. After an hour, carefully remove the eggs from their bath, and they're done.

SALTED CUCUMBERS

Makes about 3 cups, depending on the size of the cucumbers

4 Lebanese cucumbers
1 tablespoon salt

Using a Japanese mandolin, slice the cucumbers into 2 mm (1/16 inch) rounds. Put in a bowl and add the salt. Use your hands to thoroughly massage the salt into the slices. Set aside for 2 hours. When done, the cucumber slices will look limp and a lot of water will have leached out. Wash them under cold running water for a few minutes, or until they no longer taste excessively salty. Squeeze out any excess water and lay the slices out to dry on paper towels. Store in an airtight container in the fridge – they should last up to 2 days.

PICKLING LIQUID

Makes about 1.8 litres (63 fl oz)

1 litre (35 fl oz/4 cups) white vinegar
500 g (1 lb 2 oz) caster (superfine) sugar
1¼ tablespoons salt

Whisk all the ingredients together with 500 ml (17 fl oz/2 cups) water in a large bowl until the sugar and salt have completely dissolved. It will keep indefinitely.

Perfect for all kinds of vegetables, including daikon radishes, carrots and cucumbers. Simply peel the vegetable you choose and slice into batons. Put in a jar and cover with the liquid. Leave for at least a few days before using.

FRIED GARLIC CHIPS

Makes at least 1 cup

---

30 garlic cloves, peeled
vegetable oil, for deep-frying

Using a mandolin or sharp knife, slice the garlic as thinly as possible. In a heavy-based saucepan, heat the oil to 150°C (300°F). Gently add the garlic, stirring constantly. When light gold in colour, quickly scoop out the garlic with a small sieve or slotted spoon and transfer onto paper towels. Leave to cool. Garlic chips keep well in an airtight container for up to 4 days.

FRIED SHALLOTS

Makes about 2 cups

---

20 large red Asian shallots, peeled
vegetable oil, for deep-frying

Using a mandolin or sharp knife, slice the shallots thinly. In a heavy-based saucepan, heat the vegetable oil to 160°C (315°F). Add the sliced shallots, stirring constantly.

When lightly golden in colour, scoop out the slices with a small sieve, working quickly as they will continue to cook as you scoop. Drain on paper towels. Use a pair of tongs in a side-to-side motion to fluff and separate the slices. This will also help them to cool. Once completely cool, you can store them in an airtight container for up to 4 days.

An excellent condiment to keep in your spice cupboard at all times. Great for sprinkling on anything from fried chicken to tofu.

SPICY SALT

Makes about 1 cup

1 tablespoon Sichuan peppercorns
3 tablespoons coriander seeds
1 cinnamon stick
1 teaspoon cloves
2 teaspoons chilli flakes
110 g (3¾ oz) sea salt flakes
1 tablespoon Iranian sumac
1 tablespoon sugar
4 star anise
½ teaspoon white peppercorns

In a dry frypan over a medium heat, toast the Sichuan peppercorns, coriander seeds, cinnamon stick and cloves until fragrant and lightly coloured. Mix with the rest of the ingredients and blitz in a spice grinder to a fine powder. This mixture will keep in an airtight container for up to 2 months.

PORK LIVER PÂTÉ

Makes about 2 cups

800 g (1 lb 12 oz) pork livers, soaked
in milk overnight
2 tablespoons vegetable oil, for frying
3 garlic cloves, thinly sliced
125 ml (4 fl oz/¼ cup) Shaoxing wine
500 g (1 lb 2 oz) butter, chilled, chopped
into small cubes
fish sauce, to taste
ground white pepper, to taste

Drain and wash the pork livers thoroughly under cold running water. Pat dry with paper towels. Carefully trim away any veins, then dice into 2 cm (¾ inch) chunks.

In a large frying pan, heat the vegetable oil over a medium–high heat. Add the liver in batches, making sure you don't crowd the pan. Do not stir!

After 1 minute or so add the garlic. At this stage, the liver should be partially cooked, but not completely.

Deglaze the pan with the Shaoxing wine then cook out the alcohol, which should take about 3 minutes. Quickly transfer the livers to a food processor and add the butter cubes. Blitz until smooth.

Season with fish sauce and white pepper to taste. Spoon the pâté into an airtight container and smooth a piece of baking paper or plastic wrap on the surface. Put in the fridge and when it is cool enough, place the lid on the container and keep refrigerated until you're ready to use it.

NUOC CHAM

Makes about 750 ml (26 fl oz/3 cups)

---

200 ml (7 fl oz) water
200 g (7 oz) sugar
200 ml (7 fl oz) white vinegar
200 ml (7 fl oz) fish sauce
2½ tablespoons lime juice

Whisk all the ingredients together until the sugar has dissolved. Transfer to a sterilised jar and store in the fridge for up to 3 weeks.

NUOC CHAM GEL

Makes about 750 ml (26 fl oz/3 cups)

---

750 ml (26 fl oz/3 cups) nuoc cham (previous recipe)
3 g (⅛ oz) agar-agar powder
1½ tablespoons ót tuóng (following recipe)

Put the nuoc cham and agar-agar in a saucepan and whisk until combined. Bring to the boil over a high heat. Simmer for 3 minutes then pour the liquid into a shallow tray. Carefully place the tray in the fridge for the agar-agar to set.

Once cool and firm, un-mould the jelly and transfer to a blender (you can also use a hand-held blender with a bowl). Blend the jelly until a smooth gel is formed. Put in a bowl and whisk in the ót tuóng. Transfer to a squeezie bottle or a lidded container and store in the fridge where it will keep for up to 2 weeks.

ÓT TUÓNG SUBSTITUTE

Makes about ½ cup, depending on the size of the chillies

---

10 small long red chillies, coarsely chopped
3 garlic cloves
2 tablespoons white vinegar

Put the ingredients into the bowl of a food processor and blend together to make a smoothish paste. The paste will keep for up to 5 days in a jar in the fridge. You can always up the quantities to make a larger batch so you have some on hand whenever you need it.

Jellyfish usually comes dried and salted at Asian grocery stores. It gives fantastic texture to a dish and soaks up the flavours around it, making it a handy vehicle.

MARINATED JELLYFISH

Makes about 2 cups

250 g (9 oz) salted jellyfish
2½ tablespoons sugar
1¼ tablespoons salt
3½ tablespoons sesame oil
4 tablespoons red vinegar
2 tablespoons light soy sauce

Wash all the salt off the jellyfish and soak the pieces in a large container of cold water. Change the water every 6 hours or so and do this for a total of 48 hours.

If the jellyfish came whole, slice it into strips. Put it in a bowl and add the remaining ingredients. Mix well then leave to marinate for 3 hours. Freeze until needed.

COMPRESSED CELERY

Makes about 4 cups

1 bunch celery
100 ml (3½ fl oz) kombu extract

Separate the celery stalks and discard the leaves and their small branches for this recipe (you can pickle these, or use them elsewhere). So using just the thick stalks, peel the outside with a vegetable peeler and cut into 12 cm (4½ inch) lengths.

If you have a vacuum-sealer system at home, divide the celery stalks among three bags and add one- third of the kombu extract to each bag. Seal tightly and leave to marinate for at least 2 hours.

If you don't have a vacuum-sealer system use zip-lock bags, squeezing the air out of the bags as you seal them. Place the bags between two baking trays, evenly weighted on top with heavy objects such as tins of tomatoes.

This will keep for up to 4 days so make room in the fridge for this set-up.

HONG HACK
Kombu extract can be hard to come by. If you can't get it, dissolve 2 tablespoons of salt, 1 tablespoon of sugar and a splash of light soy in 100 ml (3½ fl oz) water and use that instead.

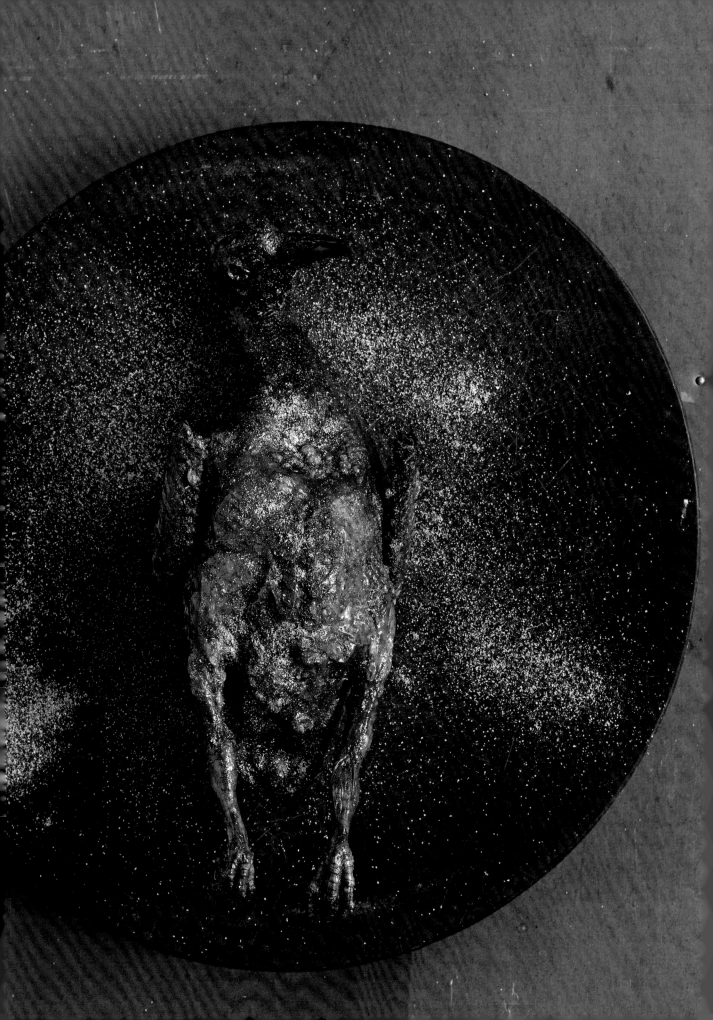

GLOSSARY

Beef balls are commonly eaten in pho. They are available from the refrigerated section of Asian grocery stores.

Black fungi is known for its rich nutrients such as iron, protein, vitamins, polysaccharides and other minerals. It is available from Asian grocery stores.

Boiler chickens are great for the basis of stocks as they have more flavour.

Chà lua is the most common type of pork loaf in Vietnamese cuisine. It is available from Vietnamese grocery stores.

Chinese rose wine is a clear sorghum liquor distilled with rock sugar and rose petals. It is primarily used in cooking, though it is also used in cocktails. It is available from Asian grocery stores.

Chipotle Peppers in Adobo Sauce are available tinned from any Latin grocery store or gourmet grocery supplier.

Chrysanthemum (tong ho) leaves are small and serrated and similar to flowering chrysanthemums, but a tad more tender. The aromatic bitter leaves are available from Asian grocery stores.

Conpoy is a dried seafood product made from the adductor muscle of the scallop. Available from Asian grocery stores. It can be very expensive, but the flavour is truly unique.

Corn nuts are also known as toasted corn. They are made of roasted and deep-fried corn kernels and are available from Asian and Latin American grocery stores.

Dried kombu (edible kelp) is a versatile ingredient that is packed full of nutrients, flavour and minerals. It can be used to make broth or added to beans to make them more digestible. It is available from Asian grocery stores.

Fuyu (fermented tofu) is a form of processed, preserved tofu that is available from Asian grocery stores.

Green papayas are available from Asian grocery stores and greengrocers.

Ice-cream stabiliser is available from confectionery stores.

Kadaifi is a shredded filo pastry available from most large supermarkets.

Knorr Liquid Seasoning is a Vietnamese kitchen staple and is available from Asian grocery stores.

Kombu extract is very hard to find, but worth looking out for. It adds a level of umami to dishes and is kind of like a natural MSG. Don't freak out if you can't find it – it's fine to omit. It is available from speciality Japanese food shops.

Kuzu is a thickener made from the starchy root of the kudzu plant. It dissolves quickly in any cold liquid and has no discernible taste. It binds more strongly than arrowroot and is available from Japanese grocery stores.

Lao Gan Ma chilli oil is a blend of oil, chilli flakes and peanuts. If the Lao Gan Ma brand is not available at your local Asian grocery store, choose another chilli paste containing peanuts.

Mango 'boba' balls are popping balls of juice.

Nuoc cham (see Essentials page 244) is a flavouring liquid.

Ót tuóng is a pickled chilli. If you can't find a jar in your Asian grocery store, there's a recipe in the Essentials section on page 244 to approximate it.

Potato starch is an excellent thickening agent and works well as a binder. It is available from health food shops and supermarkets.

Rice paddy herb is citrusy with a mild cumin flavour. It is available from Asian greengrocers.

Shichimi togarashi is a seven-flavour chilli pepper available from Japanese grocery stores.

Shio kombu is seasoned kombu cut into strips that can be substituted with rehydrated wakame, with both ingredients available from Asian grocery stores.

Shiro-dashi contains seaweed, bonito flakes (katsuoboshi), cooking sake, salt and sugar and equals instant umami. It is available from Asian grocery stores.

Shiso leaves are sometimes called perilla leaves and are available from Japanese grocery stores.

Tapioca pearls are small edible balls made from tapioca starch and are available from Asian supermarkets.

Tsubu arare are roasted rice pellets, available from Asian grocery stores.

Water chestnut flour is also known as caltrop starch and is good for making crisp coatings. It is available from Asian grocery stores.

Wheat starch is also known as non-glutinous flour. It is available from Asian grocery stores.

White soy sauce is a staple Japanese condiment available from specialist Japanese grocery stores.

Xanthan gum is a food-thickening agent available from the health food section of supermarkets.

INDEX

Page numbers in *italics* refer to photographs.

ACKNOWLEDGEMENTS

I would like to start by thanking the editorial team at Murdoch Books, and in particular Sue Hines, Corinne Roberts, Claire Grady, Barbara McClenahan, Carla Grosetti and Sophia Oravecz, for letting me realise my vision for making the kind of book that truly reflects who I am. To Terry Durack and Jill Dupleix for suggesting I write this book in the first place. To the amazing creative team, Jason Loucas (I knew you'd be right ever since our first shoot with my mum all those years ago), Hugh Ford (thank you for keeping it fun, respecting my vision and for your exceptionally bad jokes) and Matt Page for your stealth stylist moves and incredible eye for texture, colour and form. Sonia Rentsch, your imagination is insane and your creations are stunning. To Katie Choi for helping me prep for the shoot, I couldn't think of an assistant with more finesse.

A big thanks to Justin Hemmes for believing in me and giving me so many opportunities to grow. You had confidence in me before I even had the confidence in myself to achieve the impossible – your vision for Merivale is unparalleled and I am honoured to be a part of it. Thank you to Frank Roberts for being my mentor, boss and mate all at the same time. I owe so much of my restaurant knowledge to you.

Massive thanks Jowett Yu for being my right hand man for five years. I really couldn't have achieved much without you – we were such a great team! Your food knowledge cannot be matched and I wish you all the best in everything you do, my brother.

To my chef mentors, Martin Boetz, Thomas Johns, Mark Best, Pasi Petanen, Brent Savage, Tetsuya Wakuda and Martin Benn, thank you for kicking my ass when I needed it the most. To my bros, who have supported me through the years, Morgan McGlone, Darren Robertson, Mitch Orr, Clayton Wells, Adriano Zumbo, Victor Liong, Andrew Levins, Alexander Franco (thanks for the music!), Phil Wood, Luke Powell, Dan Puskas, Thomas Lim, Ben Shewry and especially my best bro, Louis Tikaram.

To my head chefs and sous chefs for running everything like a boss, Paul Donnelly, Brendan Fong, Kelvin Ng, Khanh Nguyen, Patrick Friesen, Chris Hogarth and Sergei Kulikov, as well as all of our staff, past and present, from kitchen hands to line chefs, front of house and managers.

Thank you to my dad, Le Duc Hong, for not pushing me into being a doctor or a lawyer. You were the first person to say to me 'As long as you love what you are doing, I am happy.' And I will never forget that. To my sisters, Rebecca and Francoise, thank you for your support and putting up with my annoying antics back in the day, and to Mama Fatma and Papa Bobby for your continuous support.

Melissa Leong... to be honest, I really don't know what I would have done if you said no to taking on this project. You know I can't write for shit, so thank you so much for translating my story into writing in a way that I couldn't. I could not think of anyone else to write this book with, so I am honoured that you took the time to write this with me. We're a great team and most importantly, WE DID IT!

Mum. What can I say? You are my inspiration, and one of my biggest supporters. Thank you for suggesting that I look into being a chef, for getting me my first job, for picking me up after work and for always putting up with my shit. Most importantly, thank you for making me realise I should ask Rara to marry me – you're the best mum a son could ever have.

Lastly, to my number one supporter and wife, Rara, for always believing in me and for saying yes to being my wife. Thank you for your patience, love and trust, and for understanding that the reason I work, and the reason I do anything, is for you and our daughter, Namira. You are my everything.

This edition published in 2021 by Murdoch Books, an imprint of Allen & Unwin
First published in 2014 by Murdoch Books

Murdoch Books Australia
83 Alexander Street
Crows Nest NSW 2065
Phone: +61 (0) 2 8425 0100
Fax: +61 (0) 2 9906 2218
www.murdochbooks.com.au
info@murdochbooks.com.au

Murdoch Books UK
Ormond House, 26–27 Boswell Street
London WC1N 3JZ
Phone: +44 (0) 20 8785 5995
murdochbooks.co.uk
info@murdochbooks.co.uk

For corporate orders & custom publishing, contact our business
development team at salesenquiries@murdochbooks.com.au

Publisher: Corinne Roberts
Designer and Illustrations: Hugh Ford
Photographer: Jason Loucas
Stylists: Matt Page (food) and Sonia Rentsch
Editors: Carla Grossetti and Sophia Oravecz
Food Editor: Jo Glynn
Editorial Managers: Claire Grady and Barbara McClenahan
Production Manager: Mary Bjelobrk

Text © Dan Hong and Melissa Leong 2014
The moral rights of the authors have been asserted.
Design © Murdoch Books 2014
Photography © Jason Loucas 2014

 A cataloguing-in-publication entry is available from
the catalogue of the National Library of Australia
at www.nla.gov.au.

A catalogue record for this book is available from the British Library.

Printed in China by C&C Offset Printing Co., Ltd.

ISBN 978 1 92235 159 3 AU

IMPORTANT: Those who might be at risk from the effects of salmonella poisoning (the elderly,
pregnant women, young children and those suffering from immune deficiency diseases)
should consult their doctor with any concerns about eating raw eggs.

OVEN GUIDE: You may find cooking times vary depending on the oven you are using.
For fan-forced ovens, as a general rule, set the oven temperature to 20°C (35°F) lower
than indicated in the recipe.

MEASURES GUIDE: We have used 20 ml (4 teaspoon) tablespoon measures. If you are
using a 15 ml (3 teaspoon) tablespoon add an extra teaspoon of the ingredient for
each tablespoon specified.

10 9 8 7 6 5 4 3 2